PAINS OF YOUTH

First published in 1989 by Absolute Classics, an imprint of
Absolute Press, 14 Widcombe Crescent, Bath, England

Series Editor: Giles Croft

Cover and text design: Ian Middleton

Photoset by Quadraset Ltd, Midsomer Norton
Printed by WBC Print, Bristol
Bound by W. H. Ware & Son, Clevedon
Cover printed by Stopside Print, Bath

ISBN 0 948230 17 7

PAINS OF YOUTH

Ferdinand Bruckner

Translated by Daphne Moore

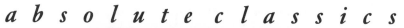

absolute classics

INTRODUCTION

In 1926 in Hamburg the world première of a new play written by a hitherto unknown young playwright was received with great acclaim. The play was KRANKHEIT DER JUGEND (PAINS OF YOUTH); the playwright, Ferdinand Bruckner. The most important theatres in Berlin, then Germany's theatre capital, had all rejected the play although many theatre insiders had been very enthusiastic about it. The director of Vienna's Raimund Theatre, Theodor Csokor, and Walter Franck, a talented young actor, had both tried to persuade Theodor Tagger to produce the play in his avantgarde Berlin Renaissance Theatre. Tagger refused, saying that he found the play too risqué, although he must have realised that it was a potential box office success which could have helped him steer his endangered theatre clear of bankruptcy. It was not until some years later when Hartung took over as Tagger's successor at the Renaissance theatre that PAINS OF YOUTH was to enjoy a tumultuously successful Berlin première.

Who was the author? The playwright never showed his face at any of the performances nor took bows at the first nights. One thing was clear – the name Ferdinand Bruckner must be a pseudonym. The author's identity was to remain a secret for some years. A second play in the same style called DIE VERBRECHER (THE CRIMINALS) was directed by Max Reinhardt at his prestigious Berlin theatre but it was not until the fantastic success of Bruckner's ELIZABETH OF ENGLAND in 1930 that the secret shared by only three others, including the author's wife and Max Reinhardt himself, was finally revealed. The same Theodor Tagger who had once vehemently refused to launch the play was the highly successful author!

The reason why Bruckner hid his identity and kept it secret for so long has never been satisfactorily explained. The sceptical say it was a trick to get around paying tax or it could have been a calculated publicity gag – in which case it paid off, since the mysterious Ferdinand Bruckner came to enjoy a much greater popularity and artistic success than his alter ego, the man of letters Theodor Tagger, who never really got his Renaissance Theatre off the ground. Or, perhaps, the use of the pseudonym was logical for someone of Tagger's self-effacing and modest personality: he was a tireless worker who penned more than fifteen Dramas and who went on to write scripts for Hollywood when in exile in America during the Nazi era.

Bruckner/Tagger was born in 1891 in Vienna as the son of an Austrian businessman and a French mother. He studied German literature in Vienna and music in Paris and Berlin. He found it hard to choose between literature and music and this dilemma is reflected in the pseudonym he adopted: the christian name refers to Ferdinand Raimund, a leading 19th century playwright, and the surname is taken from the musician, Anton Bruckner. Both were important figures for the culture of Tagger's native land, Austria.

Bruckner started writing during the First World War while working as a reader for a large publishing firm. He translated Pascal and the Psalms of David and published his own poems and essays. For a couple of years he brought out a bi-monthly journal for young literary talent and it is a tribute to his own talent as an editor that the, then unknown, writers Alfred Döblin, Gottfried Benn and Franz Werfel were among its contributors.

The greatest literary influence on Bruckner during this time was the satirist and expressionist playwright Carl Sternheim. Bruckner became a socialist and a moralist; that is, a contemporary man of literature in the Sternheim mould. In 1923 he founded the Berlin Renaissance Theatre in a converted cinema. It was one of the few Berlin theatres to survive the devastation of the Second World War and it flourishes as a successful 'literary' theatre to this day. For the Renaissance repertoire Bruckner chose mainly literary plays, most of which would now seem rather obscure.

Sternheim's influence is most prevalent in Bruckner's first play PAINS OF YOUTH. Just as Sternheim denounced pre-war Germany's philistine middle classes Bruckner is merciless with their aimless post-war children whose sense of values has been totally shaken not only by the war itself but perhaps most radically by Freud's theories which Bruckner interpreted as putting youth, sex and death in morbid proximity. Bruckner's work evolved from its expressionist roots similarly to that of Bertolt Brecht's at the same period. Both dramatists employed a staccato dialogue style and went in for sweeping emotionalism; Bruckner's young people in PAINS OF YOUTH display an amorality that we recognise again in Brecht's early heroes such as *Baal*. Although they later took entirely different paths Brecht and Bruckner retained the use of the typically expressionist diction throughout their work. The characters in PAINS OF YOUTH are all extreme in their search for real 'Life' – only death or the danger of death can bring them near enough to their goal. It is for this reason that Bruckner has sometimes been hailed as Sartre's precursor in existentialism; but his work evolved through many stages and to label him at all would be to belittle the scope of his achievement.

Of the fifteen dramas Bruckner wrote, his most successful was ELIZABETH OF ENGLAND, based on Lytton Strachey's book about Elizabeth and Essex. The play was translated into seventeen languages and performed throughout four different continents. One feature common to all Bruckner's plays is the juxtaposition of the male and female worlds. His women are the true philosophers, intrepid explorers in their quest for truth and life. Like Desirée in PAINS OF YOUTH, they may be consumed by the heat of their own fire during the course of the search but they never go against their own nature which is, in essence, motherly. Bruckner is much harder on his male characters who, for the most part, are vain and self-satisfied. These egocentric fanatics are usually imposters who tend to fizzle out.

After seventeen years in America, Bruckner returned to Berlin to assist Boleslav Barlog at his Berlin Schiller Theatre. He still wrote drama but never repeated the same successes he had had in the pre-war Berlin theatre world. On 5th December 1958, while still working on his last play, Bruckner died in a Berlin hospital.

DAPHNE MOORE

PAINS OF YOUTH was first performed in this translation at the Gate
Theatre, London in 1987. The cast was as follows:

PETRELL	Paul Mooney
ALT	Jonathan Oliver
DESIREE	Joanne Pearce
MARIE	Sylvie Rotter
IRENE	Paula Stockbridge
LUCY	Ellis Van Maarseveen
FREDER	Tim Woodward
UNDERSTUDY	Richard Lintern
DIRECTOR	Patti Love
DESIGNER	Jane Green
MUSIC	Dominic Muldowney

CHARACTERS

MARIE

DESIREE

IRENE

FREDER

PETRELL

ALT

LUCY

The girls, quite young
The men, somewhat older

Vienna, 1923

ACT ONE

All three acts take place in Marie's room in a boarding house.

SCENE ONE

DESIREE:	You're scrubbing the floor?
MARIE:	*(Marie already doing so, laughs.)* The party's on Friday.
DESIREE:	What party?
MARIE:	*(Laughs)* My graduation party. How could you forget?
DESIREE:	How could I forget? *(Exits)*
MARIE:	*(Marie at the hall door.)* Lucy, bring fresh water for the windows and a duster.
LUCY:	*(Offstage)* I'm coming.

SCENE TWO

Desiree from her room.

MARIE:	On your feet already?
DESIREE:	Come on, will you test me?
MARIE:	What time are you going up?
DESIREE:	Ten o'clock.
MARIE:	*(Cleaning the floor.)* Go ahead.
DESIREE:	The lung. *(Yawns and stretches.)* Why does one get up so early?
MARIE:	Stagefright?
DESIREE:	I don't feel anything at the moment. Right. Principally, the advanced cavernous phthisis does not differ from the normal progressive phthisis, as the formation of a cavern is only a secondary result of the caseation. *(Laughs, her legs on the table.)* Little Irene-weenie made a bet with me that she'll be qualified before me although she's two terms behind.

MARIE:	*(Still busy.)* Where do caverns appear?
DESIREE:	In the most advanced areas of infection, the superior lobes and in the subapical parts. A repulsive girl.
MARIE:	She's ambitious and beautiful.
DESIREE:	A red-headed fish. She'll go far.
MARIE:	Smaller caverns?
DESIREE:	Smaller caverns appear even by relatively minor infection. – – – Freder's after the maid.
MARIE:	*(Amazed)* Lucy?
DESIREE:	I caught him creeping out of her room.
MARIE:	What a pig. *(Desiree laughs.)* That's why she's been behaving so weirdly the last few days.
DESIREE:	*(Laughs)* And limps.
MARIE:	Lucy limps?
DESIREE:	When a woman succumbs to a man who's superior she develops another way of walking.
MARIE:	What rubbish.
DESIREE:	Fear. Repression.
MARIE:	*(Carefully)* And you?
DESIREE:	Me. I've finished with him.
MARIE:	You were crazy about each other.
DESIREE:	*(Laughs)* Once. He was the first of his sex to make me think that men are worthwhile. Right down to the very fingertips. Christ! He's not just good he's a maestro. But even maestros become boring after a while.
MARIE:	It's always boring if you don't love the man.
DESIREE:	Ah, that's what you and your soft little boy call it – love?
MARIE:	*(Laughs)* Hey, he's not so soft.
DESIREE:	*(Astonished)* No? I'd no idea he knew what a woman needs.
MARIE:	What does a woman need? *(Smiles)*
DESIREE:	*(Approaches)* Only women know what women need. *(Tenderly)* Marion. I'll call you Marion after my sister.

My happiest moments were when the governess said goodnight, turned out the light and left us alone. I'd creep into Marion's bed and we'd kiss and cuddle up and each would feel the warmth of the other body and knew what it was. The warmth of life. Since I was little, I've never felt that again.

MARIE: *(Frees herself.)* Hey, I'm not Marion.

DESIREE: Why can't we stay children for ever? Instead of being Marie you'd be my sweet little Marion.

MARIE: You long for childhood again?

DESIREE: For softness and warmth. For the padding.

MARIE: *(Frees herself.)* Not me. I'm quite happy with the present thanks. *(Working)*

DESIREE: Hey! Why all the drudgery.

MARIE: I want to celebrate in a clean place. The student days are over – it's serious living now.

DESIREE: Empty phrases. Don't kid yourself.

MARIE: If you live by them they aren't just phrases.

SCENE THREE

Lucy enters.

LUCY: I can help you now.

MARIE: Clean water for the mirror and windows please.

Lucy exits with the bucket.

DESIREE: *(Laughs)* The rivals exchange glances.

MARIE: Leave her alone.

DESIREE: Didn't you notice the side-long glance?

Lucy brings a bucket of water.

LUCY: Here's the water.

MARIE: Thanks, kid.

DESIREE: Seen Mr Freder today?

Lucy shocked, says nothing.

I'm only asking.

MARIE: Nice and clean isn't it?

LUCY: *(Blunt)* Yes.

DESIREE: You're very pretty.

Lucy looks at her wide-eyed.

MARIE: Lucy you'll see, everything's going to sparkle today.

DESIREE: Seriously. You've lovely eyes.

MARIE: The only thing missing is some music.

DESIREE: Pretty enough to fall in love with, Miss Lucy.

MARIE: A graduation party definitely needs some music.

LUCY: Room nine's away, I'll fetch his gramophone.

MARIE: You're an angel. *(Lucy exits quickly.)*

DESIREE: *(Calls after her.)* Courage Lucy. I'm your friend.
Poor cow.

MARIE: *(Cleaning the mirror.)* Go on. What about the bigger caverns?

DESIREE: Larger caverns make diagnosis more difficult because they indicate a pus reservoir. Did you notice the limp?

MARIE: The symptoms?

DESIREE: The most prevalent symptoms of caverns, not usually found simultaneously are: a) percussion 1) tympanatic ring 2) metal sound –

MARIE: When metal sound?

DESIREE: Only when the wall of the cavern is smooth and tight.

MARIE: You're wonderful. *(Desiree yawns.)* Too much talent is a sickness. Cramming is much more fun.

DESIREE: If only I could leave the unversity as easily as I left home. Things would be so much easier to bear if there was a strict father to horsewhip me, sitting on the podium and a poor dear, helpless mother crying because I'm naughty and who rushes away to the ball in her pearls. If only we could experience that again. Childhood is the only thing worth living.

MARIE: I don't want to go back. My parents hated each other.

DESIREE: Mine too, but Marion when you're a child that's fun too.
          It's only later that you start to see. People should shoot
          themselves at seventeen. *(Marie laughs.)* There's only
          disappointment after that. To avoid it all I ran away. With
          silk stockings and a very thin coat. Not a bean on me.
          (Pause. Marie works on a dress.) Your studies, your room,
          your lovers – you create them all yourself. Why all the
          exertion?

MARIE: What I find beautiful, you find superfluous. That's the
          difference.

SCENE FOUR

Lucy enters with a letter.

LUCY: A man. He's waiting outside.

DESIREE: Do you understand, Lucy? You're a very pretty girl?
          Don't be put upon.

MARIE: *(Quickly reads the letter.)* Hurry. I don't want my little boy
          to see him.

                    Exits with Lucy.

DESIREE: *(Grabs the letter.)* A bill. Little Marion plunges herself
          into debt. *(Desiree goes into her room, fetches some money
          and places it in the envelope.)*

MARIE: *(Enters, happy.)* I got rid of him. I bought my little boy a
          rococo desk. He said he could write much better on an
          antique. Inspiration, you understand –

DESIREE: *(Laughs)* You're an idiot.

MARIE: *(Throws the envelope away and discovers the money.)* You?

DESIREE: *(Hugs her.)* Little Marion.

MARIE: I won't take it.

DESIREE: Idiot. *(Kisses her.)* Huh! Because you're in love with a
          man? I'll have to take care of you.

MARIE: Crazy girl.

DESIREE: A child just like you, because I'm also in love. With you.

MARIE: Let go.

DESIREE: *(Laughs wildly.)* I'll not let go. I'll not let you go. If you
            promise me.

MARIE: *(Pushes her away.)* *(Pause)* We won't talk about it
            any more.

DESIREE: *(Pale)* Marion.

MARIE: Poor bitch. *(Sits and sews.)* Right. Symptoms when
            percussion: second metal sound, third?

DESIREE: *(Looks at her and turns to go to her door.)*

MARIE: Desy, your money.

DESIREE: *(Takes the money and goes to her room.)*

MARIE: *(Watches her. Pause. Goes to the door.)* You ought to be
            ashamed of yourself. Dumb kid. *(Tries to open the door.)*
            Open the door. I didn't mean to hurt you. Open up, Desy.

SCENE FIVE

Freder.

MARIE: *(Nervously)* You?

FREDER: I must see Desy. The door's closed.

MARIE: This one here as well.

FREDER: Ah, ha!

MARIE: These things are none of your business.

FREDER: *(Watches her.)*

MARIE: *(Nervous)* Your presence was never particularly pleasant
            to me. I like to be frank, Mr Freder. *(Folds the dress.)*

FREDER: The graduation frock? My congratulations.

MARIE: *(Marie says nothing.)*

FREDER: You've achieved more in ten terms here than I have in
            twenty. But still: we're kindred spirits.

MARIE: Athlete.

FREDER: *(Laughs)* Where are the barbarians of the twentieth

century, asks Nietzsche? And quite right too. Here
I stand before you.

MARIE: Try for a job at the fun-fair.

FREDER: Without the 'strongmen' – I wonder what life would be
            like?

MARIE: Why don't you go and hang yourself?

FREDER: You'll want me, sooner or later.

MARIE: Drunk at this time of the morning.

FREDER: Why not?

MARIE: Animal.

FREDER: You just can't ignore me. Ask Desy.

MARIE: She despises you.

FREDER: Not in bed, my angel.

MARIE: What? How dare you.

FREDER: First let Ireny-weenie get to grips with little boy blue.

MARIE: Irene?

FREDER: The sterile little bitch.

MARIE: He's not little boy blue but Mr Petrell to you.

FREDER: I like him.

MARIE: I wasn't asking.

FREDER: A dreamer, a sweet little good for nothing. He'd make a
            woman go broody in bed.

MARIE: Have you anything more to say?

FREDER: I'm very understanding. *(Takes out a bottle of brandy.)*
            My congratulations.

MARIE: It wasn't necessary. *(Nervous)*

FREDER: Indeed. Why do we need doctors at all in this decadent
            age? The more sickness there is, the more superfluous the
            medics. But you still drudge away to save baby boy blue's
            skin. And your own. There's a better remedy for despair
            than working.

MARIE: You can be sure I'll follow your example.

FREDER:	Take it in your hands and sling it back. Why do you hate me?
MARIE:	You're right.
FREDER:	It's downright dangerous.
MARIE:	*(Laughs)*
FREDER:	Dangerous to hate a person that much.
MARIE:	I don't hate you.
FREDER:	That remains to be seen.
MARIE:	You're very opinionated.
FREDER:	*(Laughs)* Quite right.

SCENE SIX

Desiree wearing a hat.

MARIE:	*(Quickly)* I'll walk you to college.
DESIREE:	*(Laughs at Freder.)*
FREDER:	We are going 'up' today, duchess?
DESIREE:	You're looking better.
FREDER:	Shake hands.
MARIE:	I'll take your jacket.
DESIREE:	Reeking of alcohol at this hour.
FREDER:	You abandoned me.
DESIREE:	Consolation wasn't hard to find.
FREDER:	That kind of consolation isn't worth much.
DESIREE:	Pining after me?
FREDER:	No man could forget you.
MARIE:	*(Impatient, to Desiree.)* Are you coming?
DESIREE:	*(Laughs)* Good heavens! *(Exits, Marie follows.)*

SCENE SEVEN

Lucy

FREDER:	*(Calmly)* Lucy.
LUCY:	*(Still)* I have to take the water away.
FREDER:	What water?
LUCY:	*(Points at the bucket.)* That there, Mr Freder.
FREDER:	You're lying. When people fetch buckets they don't creep . . . Come here. What do you want?
LUCY:	*(Afraid and helpless.)* Mr Freder.
FREDER:	Shall I tell you what?
LUCY:	You're hurting me.
FREDER:	Where? I'm not touching you.
	Lucy: silent.
	Where am I hurting you?
LUCY:	*(Cries)*
FREDER:	When you saw the others go out together, you wanted to be alone with me, didn't you?
LUCY:	*(Softly)* Yes.
FREDER:	Have courage when you want something. Fetching water's a lie, but –
LUCY:	You're hurting me.
FREDER:	Where for God's sake? I'm not touching you.
LUCY:	*(Sobs)*
FREDER:	*(More gently.)* Come, come you're a good girl.
LUCY:	*(Looks at him with big eyes, and goes to him.)* Mr Freder.
FREDER:	*(Strokes her hair.)* A good girl. *(Draw her down to him and hits her playfully on the back.)* My doggy.
LUCY:	Yes.
FREDER:	My little pet.
LUCY:	Yes, yes.

FREDER:	*(Lifts her face.)* Look in my eyes. *(Pause)* Beautiful clear eyes.
LUCY:	*(Softly)* Yes.
FREDER:	*(Kisses her eyes.)* Did nobody ever tell you that?
LUCY:	*(Softly)* No.
FREDER:	Could you sleep yesterday, after I left you?
LUCY:	*(Shakes her head.)*
FREDER:	Why not?
LUCY:	*(Smiles)* Mr Freder.
FREDER:	*(Strokes her hair.)* Love me?
LUCY:	Don't ask.
FREDER:	*(Draws her to him.)*
LUCY:	*(Unresisting)* Mr Freder.
FREDER:	*(Kisses her.)* My sweet little girl.
LUCY:	*(Unresisting)* If someone comes.
FREDER:	I'm very fond of you.
LUCY:	*(Kisses his hand nearly in tears.)* Ah!
FREDER:	Tell me.
LUCY:	I can't –
FREDER:	*(Softly)* And this morning?
LUCY:	*(Nods)*
FREDER:	Go on. Did you manage?
LUCY:	*(Nods)*
FREDER:	And?
LUCY:	*(Softly)* The two rings.
FREDER:	Mrs Schimmelbrot's?
LUCY:	*(Nods)*
FREDER:	Was she still sleeping?
LUCY:	*(Nods)*

FREDER: Are you sure she didn't notice?

LUCY: Not a thing.

FREDER: Go on.

LUCY: I can't.

FREDER: Where were the rings?

LUCY: In the cupboard on the second shelf.

FREDER: You knew that?

LUCY: She always hides her jewellery there.

FREDER: Did you light a candle?

LUCY: It was practically dawn.

FREDER: It was already light?

LUCY: There was enough from the cracks in the blinds.

FREDER: Did you go to her bed first?

LUCY: Like you told me to.

FREDER: How near?

LUCY: To the bedside table.

FREDER: What was on the bedside table?

LUCY: A glass of water and some hairpins.

FREDER: Mrs Schimmelbrot's?

LUCY: *(Nods)*

FREDER: These kind of hairpins? *(Undoes her hair.)*

LUCY: *(Unresisting)* Mr Freder.

FREDER: *(Kisses her hair.)* It smells wonderful.

LUCY: If someone comes.

FREDER: Look in my eyes. Beautiful eyes. *(Kisses her eyes.)*

LUCY: Mr Freder.

FREDER: Where are the rings?

LUCY: Under my pillow.

FREDER: Someone might find them.

LUCY: *(Afraid)* Shall I fetch them?

FREDER:	Hide them in the dining room.
LUCY:	*(Nods)*
FREDER:	Under the dresser.
LUCY:	*(Nods)*
FREDER:	Get up.
LUCY:	*(Frees herself from Freder.)*
FREDER:	I'll come to you again tonight.
LUCY:	*(Nearly breathless.)* Yes.
FREDER:	We'll make love again.
LUCY:	Yes.
FREDER:	What kind of rings are they?
LUCY:	I didn't look at them.
FREDER:	Gold?
LUCY:	I don't know.
FREDER:	And Mrs Schimmelbrot didn't notice?
LUCY:	She's still sleeping.
FREDER:	And if she finds out?
LUCY:	She doesn't often wear the rings.
FREDER:	She must notice sometime.
LUCY:	*(Unconcerned)* I don't know. *(Suddenly)* Nobody'd think of you.
FREDER:	What's it got to do with me?
LUCY:	*(Quickly)* Nothing – And even if they kill me, nobody'll ever find out about you.
FREDER:	What the hell, what do you mean? It was your idea.
LUCY:	Yes. It was my idea.
FREDER:	What's it got to do with me? Tidy your hair.
LUCY:	*(Tidies it.)*
FREDER:	I want to help you.
LUCY·	Mr Freder.

FREDER:	*(Embraces her.)*
LUCY:	*(Unresisting)* If someone comes.
FREDER:	Mrs Schimmelbrot perhaps?
LUCY:	Mr Freder.
FREDER:	Why are you shaking?
LUCY:	I'm not afraid for myself.
FREDER:	*(Lets go of her.)* That remains to be seen.
LUCY:	I'm not afraid for myself.
FREDER:	You wanted to fetch the water?
LUCY:	What water?
FREDER:	*(Points at the bucket.)* That there.
LUCY:	*(Motionless)* Yes.
FREDER:	Take it away.
LUCY:	*(Motionless)* Yes.
FREDER:	And the rings.
LUCY:	*(Wakens)* Yes, underneath the dresser.
FREDER:	For me to find.
LUCY:	On the right, under the carpet.
FREDER:	On the right, under the carpet. Take the bucket with you.
LUCY:	*(Takes the bucket.)*
FREDER:	Hurry up.
LUCY:	Mr Freder.
FREDER:	Is it too heavy for you?
LUCY:	No.
FREDER:	Do you want me to help you?
LUCY:	*(Quickly)* No.
FREDER:	*(Goes to Desiree's door.)* I'll stretch myself out in here.
LUCY:	*(Startled)* Yes.
FREDER:	Jealous?
LUCY:	*(Silent)*

FREDER:	Of Desiree? Don't forget that she's a duchess.
LUCY:	*(Violently)* A runaway duchess.
FREDER:	*(Laughs)* Damn!
LUCY:	At seventeen already –
FREDER:	And you?
LUCY:	*(Silent)*
FREDER:	Well then, keep your mouth shut.
LUCY:	Every night lying there –
FREDER:	Don't spill the water.
LUCY:	I hate her. I'd rather be –
FREDER:	Shut your mouth.
LUCY:	Mr Freder.
FREDER:	I'll go and stretch myself out. *(Goes into Desiree's room.)*
LUCY:	*(Softly)* Mr Freder.

SCENE EIGHT

Irene and Petrell.

PETRELL:	No one here?
LUCY:	Miss has examinations today. *(Exits)*
IRENE:	*(Laughs)* Desiree and her examinations.
PETRELL:	*(Stretches out.)* Marie'll have kept her company.
IRENE:	Make yourself at home little boy.
PETRELL:	*(Laughs)*
IRENE:	Marie calls you that.
PETRELL:	I'm just a plaything for Marie.
IRENE:	All of us are, little boy.
PETRELL:	Stop saying that.
IRENE:	He can be cross too?
PETRELL:	It's getting on my nerves.

IRENE:	I won't say it again – then again everything she does is useless and superfluous.
PETRELL:	Who?
IRENE:	Desiree. Amateurish.
PETRELL:	She managed to get her matriculation just by cramming for a year with a stupid tutor.
IRENE:	Thanks to Alt, who spent endless nights drumming it into her.
PETRELL:	She still passes the most difficult things with distinction.
IRENE:	Because she's a Countess. She's no idea what real work is.
PETRELL:	Don't upset yourself.
IRENE:	We poor underdogs have to drudge our way to the top. Nobody sees us in the shadows. Even in Science it's nearly always the charlatan and not the worker who finally attains the laurels.
PETRELL:	Creative man is a charlatan.
IRENE:	*(Laughs)*
PETRELL:	Very good. That suits you.
IRENE:	She's two semesters ahead of me. Just wait and see who graduates first. Bah! She doesn't interest me.
PETRELL:	Don't get excited then.
IRENE:	It's all bluff. We all know what's in her mind. Any prostitute on the street is preferable. At least she's honest about what she does.
PETRELL:	You want to be a doctor?
IRENE:	I refuse to be impressed by Duchesses and coronets. She'll come to a bad end.
PETRELL:	Who'll come to a bad end?
IRENE:	Desiree.
PETRELL:	*(Nods)* Now you're talking sense.
IRENE:	I've no pity. She should have stayed well at home with Daddy the Duke.
PETRELL:	What's her father do?

IRENE: At the moment that's not the issue.

PETRELL: *(Laughs)* What is the issue then?

IRENE: We'll discuss it this time next year.

PETRELL: Next year –

IRENE: – she'll have gone the way of all melancholy coquettes.
            She'll end up in an opium den.

PETRELL: *(Laughs)* For God's sake.

IRENE: Or in a funeral parlour.

PETRELL: Why are you always so bitter?

IRENE: Basically, I'm perfectly indifferent.

PETRELL: Well then.

IRENE: Nobody fools me that's all.

PETRELL: You envy her the lovers?

IRENE: *(Laughs angrily.)* Perhaps Freder?

PETRELL: How old are you? You're very young. You're also very
            pretty. Why do you always show your claws?

IRENE: *(Laughs)* Ah, go on!

PETRELL: You really are very pretty but one hardly has the courage
            to say so.

IRENE: Desiree makes it much easier.

PETRELL: What do you get out of it?

IRENE: I'm serious about my profession, that's all. Women who
            study can't be whores at the same time. It sullies the
            name of the medical profession.

PETRELL: The profession should be as pure as the driven snow?

IRENE: Little boy.

PETRELL: To be without someone means that you stay pure?

IRENE: *(Silenced)*

PETRELL: No one gets close to you.

IRENE: Science demands absolute entirety. That means loneliness
            if you like.

PETRELL: Empty words.

IRENE:	*(Smiles)* Little boy –
PETRELL:	Right, you can call me little boy. It's something else. Inhibitions.
IRENE:	Don't talk nonsense.
PETRELL:	It's an inferiority complex. You should fight it. You're known to be proud and unapproachable. But pride is repressed insecurity. You are shy and afraid.
IRENE:	*(Laughs)* Write a story about it.
PETRELL:	If anybody dared to touch you, you'd strike them dead. You've never had a man. Right?
IRENE:	*(Silent)*
PETRELL:	I don't believe in frigid women: you're simply scared.
IRENE:	For God's sake shut up.
PETRELL:	Just because a woman allows a little tenderness doesn't mean she's a whore.
IRENE:	Just write it all down. You may need it for the new rococo desk.
PETRELL:	*(Beside her.)* Why so scornful?
IRENE:	Because I could die laughing.
PETRELL:	*(Carefully fondles her hair.)* You're beautiful, Irene.
IRENE:	*(Motionless)* Stop playing.
PETRELL:	*(Uncertain)* I'm not playing.
IRENE:	Take your hand away.
PETRELL:	I don't want to. *(Puts his arms around her.)*
IRENE:	*(Motionless)* Little boy.
PETRELL:	Poor little self-persecuted girl.
IRENE:	*(Softly)* Let me go. Remember Marie.
PETRELL:	Marie can't see us. *(Embraces her.)*
IRENE:	*(Tries to free herself.)* Mr Petrell.
PETRELL:	You trickster. You're game for anything.
IRENE:	*(Frees herself.)* I don't want stolen love.
PETRELL:	Empty phrases.

IRENE: You're exploiting our situation.

PETRELL: The only thing I can say is tut, tut, tut!

IRENE: You've mistaken your woman.

PETRELL: Let me remedy that.

IRENE: Ask Marie's permission first.

PETRELL: You're a little beast.

IRENE: She's a lioness who protects her young. Don't goad her.

PETRELL: I'm not her son.

IRENE: *(Laughs)* Little boy.

PETRELL: I'm free to do as I please.

IRENE: *(Laughs)* Little boy.

PETRELL: Don't entice me.

IRENE: You'd have better ideas at the rococo desk Mammie
           bought you.

PETRELL: Stop it.

IRENE: *(Laughter increases.)* This association – inspiration with
           pieces of furniture. Sickening. But that's the mentality of
           students today. A melancholy coquette and a peasant girl
           from Passau.

PETRELL: Jealous of Marie too? I feel sorry for you.

IRENE: I don't mean you. With discipline and training you could
           have gone places.

PETRELL: I'm not ambitious.

IRENE: You're lying. You write appallingly. But sometimes there
           are a few lines where a little bit of individuality shows
           through. It's a pity about that.

PETRELL: You really read my stuff then?

IRENE: It's a shame really.

PETRELL: I'm still young.

IRENE: You could win power and fame.

PETRELL: *(Ironically)* Power and fame.

IRENE: Go on, laugh. The truth is, the inspirationally creative are
           actually devoured by secret ambition.

PETRELL: I'm not entirely devoured yet.

IRENE: You're a nobody. You're still tied to your mama's apron
            strings. What do you know about desperate lonely nights
            and torturous hours of work. You little lover's mummy's
            boy!

PETRELL: Is that sarcasm or are you serious?

IRENE: Very serious.

PETRELL: *(Pause)* Very serious?

IRENE: *(Softly)* Yes.

PETRELL: Irene.

IRENE: Don't touch me.

PETRELL: You confuse me.

IRENE: Poor little boy. *(Laughs)* Keep your hands to yourself.
            Do you always have to touch a woman when you think
            she's on your side?

PETRELL: You're on my side?

IRENE: *(Suddenly)* Someone's coming.

PETRELL: *(Opens Desiree's door.)* Mr Freder.

IRENE: *(Shocked)* Mr Freder?

FREDER: *(From inside.)* You may enter, Petrell.

PETRELL: Miss Irene is here. Don't disturb yourself. *(Shuts the door.)*

IRENE: *(Quickly)* He heard us.

PETRELL: He's lying on the couch at the other end of the room.

IRENE: Beware of him.

PETRELL: You're suspicious of everyone.

IRENE: I've got my head screwed on.

PETRELL: Denying yourself every pleasure in life.

IRENE: *(Laughs)* Pleasure?

PETRELL: Pleasure! Heard of it?

IRENE: Desperate loneliness. When creative – it's the sole
            pleasure in life.

PETRELL: Hermit.

IRENE:	I think we misunderstand one another. How long have you known Marie?
PETRELL:	Two years.
IRENE:	At the time –
PETRELL:	Still at university, a student who hated studying. Marie made life good. I've a lot to thank her for.
IRENE:	*(Unappreciatively)* At least you're grateful to her.
PETRELL:	But for her I would have died of starvation. Literally starvation.
IRENE:	At the mother's breast.
PETRELL:	*(Angry)* You're disgusting.
IRENE:	Reasonable people are always called disgusting when they're discerning. You'd be another man today, if Marie –
PETRELL:	I would have died of hunger.
IRENE:	Nobody dies of hunger. Just before you pop off, you wake up and discover who you are. I had no mother's milk and didn't die.
PETRELL:	You've had a dog's life.
IRENE:	*(Laughs)* Thank God!
PETRELL:	I don't envy you.
IRENE:	Yes. But then I'm unbeatable.

SCENE NINE

Freder enters.

FREDER:	*(Laughs)* A little plot?
IRENE:	*(Picks up a book.)*
PETRELL:	We're waiting for Marie.
FREDER:	Exactly.
PETRELL:	*(Stretches himself out.)*
FREDER:	Have you had a good look?

PETRELL: No.

FREDER: Spick and span from top to bottom. The graduation's to
            be a real birthday party.

PETRELL: Let her have her fun.

FREDER: Health, happiness and a long life.

PETRELL: Cheers.

FREDER: Your Marie is a Sunday's child.

PETRELL: The profession proclaims there's no such thing as health.

FREDER: The profession is reading a new book. Do not disturb.

IRENE: No comment. *(Reads)*

FREDER: Well. It was precisely your voice that woke me up just
            now.

IRENE: I always imagined you'd eavesdrop.

FREDER: And peep through keyholes.

PETRELL: *(Uncomfortable)* Really?

FREDER: *(Looks at him.)* Certainly.

IRENE: *(Quickly)* We've nothing to hide.

FREDER: Nothing I don't already know about.

IRENE: *(Laughs)* Don't let yourself be cowed, Mr Petrell.

FREDER: Little boy.

PETRELL: What do you mean, little boy?

FREDER: Little girl.

IRENE: You're drunk. *(Reads)*

FREDER: Weren't you both playing little boys and girls just now?

IRENE: *(Stands up.)* Come with me, Mr Petrell.

FREDER: A pretty young man, our little boy.

PETRELL: *(Stands up.)* We were waiting for Marie.

IRENE: We can do that downstairs.

FREDER: *(Laughs)* What would she think!

IRENE: That your presence drove us out.

FREDER:	But little girl.
IRENE:	Come.
PETRELL:	This is nonsense.
FREDER:	I'm waiting for Desiree.
IRENE:	Desiree's room is next door.
FREDER:	So I'm told.
IRENE:	This is ridiculous *(Sits down.)*
FREDER:	*(Pause)* What are you reading? *(Stretches himself out.)*
IRENE:	*(Silent)*
FREDER:	Make yourself at home, Mr Petrell. I've taken your seat.
PETRELL:	Stay where you are.
FREDER:	If only she weren't so malicious.
PETRELL:	You shouldn't provoke her.
FREDER:	Such a pretty girl.
IRENE:	Keep your tasteless remarks to yourself.
FREDER:	*(Laughs)* You're on form again.
PETRELL:	Perhaps Marie'll wait 'til the exam's over.
FREDER:	Hardly.
IRENE:	I can tell you in advance, Petrell: Desiree will fly through.
FREDER:	Desiree flies through all kinds of things.
IRENE:	*(Scornful)* You should know.
FREDER:	She's a fine fellow in every sense of the word.
IRENE:	Spare us the details.
FREDER:	Now that was in bad taste. *(Laughs)*
IRENE:	*(Reads)*
FREDER:	And what little surprise have you in store for Marie?
PETRELL:	I haven't had time yet.
FREDER:	*(Points to the brandy bottle.)* From me.
IRENE:	Marie is teetotal.
FREDER:	Little boy must rid her of those scruples.

IRENE:	Meanwhile she's teaching them to him.
FREDER:	Agreed, little girl.
IRENE:	Keep quiet.
PETRELL:	Marie is in fact so healthy –
IRENE:	What's that?
FREDER:	Bravo. There's no such thing as health.
IRENE:	At any rate youth is never healthy. The spirit still sleeps in a dream.
PETRELL:	*(Softly)* Youth sleeps in a dream. That's beautiful, Irene.
IRENE:	You fall in love with words. Youth is a tumour. Youth is latent proximity to death.
PETRELL:	Youth is the only adventure in our lives.
FREDER:	You're only interrupting to say the same.
IRENE:	To match the rococo desk.
PETRELL:	Irene.
IRENE:	*(Swiftly)* I beg your pardon.
PETRELL:	Fantastic, Novalis said: 'Nothing differentiates man from nature more than the fact that he is condemned to love pain and sickness.'
IRENE:	Novalis was neurotic.
PETRELL:	*(Still enthusiastic.)* Condemned, we are condemned.
IRENE:	He's a poet.
FREDER:	*(Smoking)* I'm just about to make an interesting experiment.
PETRELL:	*(Softly)* Poet. I don't know if I'm a poet.
FREDER:	An interesting experiment. I'm about to bring a person to the point of committing a theft for me.
PETRELL:	You're a menace to society.
FREDER:	All science is a menace to society.
IRENE:	You are not a scientist.
FREDER:	Unfortunately one discovers that much too late.

IRENE: *(Excited)* I think you're –

FREDER: *(Sitting upright.)* Keep on talking.

IRENE: Rather not.

FREDER: Courage, little girl.

IRENE: I think you're criminal.

FREDER: *(Laughs)* That's the profession.

IRENE: You have no profession.

FREDER: You're excited because you're afraid of me.

IRENE: Megalomaniac.

FREDER: Afraid. You know well enough, my way's the only way. To be creative, means to be in danger. Not just in theory, little girl. You don't get knowledge from leafing through manuals with wet fingers. But you're very wary.

IRENE: I'm wary of you because one day you'll end up behind bars.

FREDER: All genius should be locked up.

IRENE: That's ridiculous.

FREDER: You cling to books because your little nose smells danger. You know quite well what's involved. My respects, little brain.

IRENE: I can't listen to this any more.

FREDER: *(To Petrell.)* I've already half seduced her.

IRENE: *(Wild)* Leave the boy alone.

FREDER: *(Laughs)* Little boy.

IRENE: Nothing's sacred to you.

FREDER: Little boy might be corrupted.

PETRELL: Corrupted?

IRENE: Don't pay any attention.

FREDER: Pay no attention little boy.

IRENE: I'm not listening either.

FREDER: Now you're lying.

IRENE: *(Turns away.)*

FREDER:	Shall I tell you about my experiment?
IRENE:	We don't want to be your accomplices in crime thanks.
FREDER:	Tonight at eleven, if no one sees us.
PETRELL:	Why provoke her?
FREDER:	Between ourselves, purely scientifically.
IRENE:	Don't answer him.
PETRELL:	You're cruel.
FREDER:	I'm doing research.
PETRELL:	Right now?
FREDER:	That astounds you, what little boy?
IRENE:	A lot of nonsense.
FREDER:	Even in the sciences knowledge must first be made valid by the experience of doing.
IRENE:	All nonsense.
FREDER:	*(Laughs)* Said Goethe.
PETRELL:	*(Astonished)* Goethe?
FREDER:	He didn't just write the Erlkönig, or shouldn't baby boy know that either.
IRENE:	*(To Petrell.)* Do you want to stay here much longer?
FREDER:	Don't make a scene, my pigeon. You can manage quite well without. You're healthier than all of us. Even healthier than sturdy Marie. The big difference is – you know the dangers.
PETRELL:	Let's talk about something else.
FREDER:	Quiet. She's enjoying it. He who lets the law set the limits for research shall grow old and become a bureaucrat. You'll definitely make a good bureaucrat, Miss.
PETRELL:	Enough.
FREDER:	I'll never even make a doctor.
PETRELL:	Just take your time.
FREDER:	Twelve years.

PETRELL:	Twelve years. The romance of the eternal student.
FREDER:	You're an idiot – I beg your pardon.
PETRELL:	*(Laughs)* Please.
FREDER:	If I were a woman, I could fall in love with you like little girl.
PETRELL:	Miss Irene isn't in love with me.
FREDER:	Close your ears little boy. Your baby charms would set any woman pleasantly in heat, and you know it. Wasn't Desy ever in love with you?
IRENE:	*(Full of attention.)*
PETRELL:	Never!
FREDER:	I'm not jealous.
PETRELL:	No, never.
FREDER:	You could make even Desy go broody.

SCENE TEN

Alt.

FREDER:	*(Stretches himself out.)*
ALT:	Our honourable doctor isn't home?
PETRELL:	Desiree goes up today.
FREDER:	Petrell, give me a cigarette.
ALT:	*(Softly)* Is that so?
IRENE:	*(Uncertain)* What?
ALT:	Watch out.
IRENE:	*(Laughs)* I don't understand you.
FREDER:	*(To Petrell.)* That's interesting. Desiree –
PETRELL:	Shall I swear?
FREDER:	All women take a shine to you.
PETRELL:	Desiree hardly looks at me.
FREDER:	She's had too many flops with delicate youths.

ALT:	I won't allow it.
IRENE:	You're dreaming.
ALT:	She'll find out.
IRENE:	I'm not afraid of a farmer's daughter.
FREDER:	You like to play the sceptic, but you're not one at all.
PETRELL:	I can't fathom you.
FREDER:	It's her feminine weapon. *(Points)* Little girl's weapon is her pride.
PETRELL:	Don't say little girl.
FREDER:	*(Laughs)* You're quickly disillusioned.
PETRELL:	What are you getting at?
FREDER:	You believe in words. Ideals on pedestals mustn't be called little girl.
IRENE:	That's none of your business.
ALT:	It's not your business to go to his room.
IRENE:	I'm truly sorry for anyone with such a filthy mind.
ALT:	What were you looking for in his room so early this morning?
IRENE:	I wanted to see the rococo desk. *(Laughs)*
FREDER:	Marie's weapon is her robust health. Others use their weakness. But basically we're all the same. All poor devils.
PETRELL:	I'd actually like to go home.
FREDER:	Work.
PETRELL:	You guess everything.
FREDER:	The new desk.
PETRELL:	Now you're being sarcastic again.
FREDER:	Small things inspire great intentions. But real staying power is something else.
PETRELL:	I want to write a great novel.
FREDER:	You're instantly inspired?
PETRELL:	You would play the main part.

FREDER:	*(Laughs)*
IRENE:	I was hardly three minutes up there, I just went to call for him.
ALT:	Now you're worried.
IRENE:	If every harmless –
ALT:	It wasn't harmless.
IRENE:	You think –
ALT:	Your intention wasn't harmless.
IRENE:	I feel sorry for you.

<u>SCENE ELEVEN</u>

MARIE:	*(Enters)* Alt? How lovely. *(Takes off her hat and coat.)*
ALT:	For she's a jolly good fellow.
FREDER:	And so say all of us.
PETRELL:	*(Softly)* Now I know.
IRENE:	What?
PETRELL:	Freder said so.
IRENE:	Be quiet.
PETRELL:	You're in love with me.
IRENE:	Be quiet here.
ALT:	Where's Desiree?
IRENE:	Passing, with flying colours.
MARIE:	I only went as far as the gate.
FREDER:	Happy for her if she failed at last.
MARIE:	So subdued, little boy?
IRENE:	Desiree is on your conscience.
ALT:	Every one has something.
IRENE:	You don't conduct operations in silk stockings.
FREDER:	Why not?

PETRELL:	By the way, thanks for the desk.
MARIE:	When did it arrive?
PETRELL:	Early this morning, I was still asleep.
MARIE:	Beautiful isn't it?
PETRELL:	Very beautiful, they had to wake me up.
MARIE:	Happy?
PETRELL:	Beautiful, too beautiful.
MARIE:	You'll soon get used to it.
PETRELL:	Yes.
MARIE:	Is something wrong? – Where are you going to put it?
PETRELL:	In the room.
MARIE:	*(Laughs)* So I imagined – Come on.
PETRELL:	What?
MARIE:	Why are you so cross?
PETRELL:	Nothing important.
MARIE:	Come on, tell.
PETRELL:	*(Vehemently)* Don't cross examine me.
MARIE:	*(Laughs)* You.
PETRELL:	My own mother was bad enough.
MARIE:	Out of sorts, little boy?
PETRELL:	The lover's mummy's boy – that's too much.
IRENE:	*(Listening intently.)* Are we in the way?
PETRELL:	How dare you?
IRENE:	We can always go.
FREDER:	*(Explodes)* Thalatta, Thalatta!
IRENE:	What did you say?
FREDER:	Thalatta, Thalatta!
ALT:	Let him enjoy himself.
FREDER:	That's the Greek war cry. Didn't you go to school?
IRENE:	Very amusing.

FREDER:	The battle begins.
IRENE:	Delirium tremens.
FREDER:	Forward march, take position, little boy in the middle.
MARIE:	Stop this nonsense.
FREDER:	Forward march, little girl. We want to be in on it.
MARIE:	Who's little girl?
FREDER:	Miss Irene.
IRENE:	Be quiet.
FREDER:	May I introduce little boy's little girl. *(Whistles, Alt holds Irene back.)*
ALT:	She'll scratch your eyes out.
FREDER:	*(Whistles)* Come on then.
MARIE:	*(She goes to Freder.)*
FREDER:	Don't get excited, Sunday's child.
MARIE:	How dare you?
FREDER:	Take care of your young man.
MARIE:	Out.
FREDER:	Or break it up. *(Puts his arms around Marie.)* He's not your type.
MARIE:	*(Tears herself away.)* You lout!
FREDER:	One on the backside. This sterile apparatus.
IRENE:	I don't have to stand for this. *(Goes)*
FREDER:	*(Laughs)* Indeed she does.
MARIE:	Children?
PETRELL:	We should bring her back. *(Goes quickly.)*
MARIE:	*(Amazed)* No.
FREDER:	*(Whistles softly.)*
MARIE:	What's going on? *(Exits)*
ALT:	This is all your fault.
FREDER:	*(Looks at Alt. Pause.)* I think she prefers you, Mr Alt. *(Exit)*

MARIE:	*(Enters quickly.)* They're already downstairs. *(Takes her hat and coat.)*
ALT:	Two steps at a time.
MARIE:	*(Laughs)* Can you explain that to me?
ALT:	What?
MARIE:	I'll catch them up.
ALT:	*(Severely)* Hardly. Come and sit down.
MARIE:	*(Looks at him in astonishment.)*
ALT:	Marie, over here.
MARIE:	I don't understand you.
ALT:	Let them run.
MARIE:	They're not running. They're on the street.
ALT:	Perhaps they're running even on the street.
MARIE:	*(Relaxing)*
ALT:	Sit down beside me.
MARIE:	*(Motionless)*
ALT:	Take off your hat.
MARIE:	*(Complies mechanically.)*
ALT:	Jacket as well.
MARIE:	*(Sits down, after a while.)* You're seeing things.
ALT:	Make yourself comfortable, we've all the time in the world.
MARIE:	No my dear, she's not worth thinking about.
ALT:	One's never ruined by something worthwhile.
MARIE:	It's all not true.
ALT:	I lost my job at the general hospital, was many years in prison. A dying child was suffering so much, I decided to shorten his agony. I gave him morphia instead of camphor, are you listening?
MARIE:	Morphia instead of camphor.
ALT:	My career was ruined and I'd do it again. Do you understand?

MARIE: You'd do it again.

ALT: I would do it again.

MARIE: You'd do it again. *(Laughs)* No that's not serious.

ALT: Nothing about a little boy's serious.

MARIE: I'm supposed to suddenly tear him out of my heart?

ALT: Imprisoned for manslaughter. Two years. You would have done the same.

MARIE: What?

ALT: It shows how obsolete the law is.

MARIE: I'm going mad.

ALT: We live behind the times. Just imagine it. Do you understand?

MARIE: Just imagine it? *(Laughs)* He's probably with her at this very minute.

ALT: Clench your fists.

MARIE: *(Mechanically)* Clench your fists.

ALT: Come to your senses.

MARIE: Come to your senses.

ALT: Wake up. Hanging on to other people is weak.

MARIE: To live like Freder is strong.

ALT: In the full consciousness of your own self.

MARIE: In full consciousness. *(Laughs)* We're both raving mad.

ALT: Now you've come to reason.

MARIE: Now I've come to reason.

ALT: Eradicate him from your mind.

MARIE: Animal, like Freder.

ALT: Freder isn't an animal.

MARIE: A criminal.

ALT: Me too?

MARIE: *(Astonished)* You? – She's with him now.

ALT: With him.

MARIE: With him? *(Her laughter increases.)*   And hardly an hour ago I was scrubbing the floor. For whom? Laugh. A spotless room. *(Takes the bottle beside her and hurls it at the mirror.)* How it shatters. Did you hear the noise? No spotless room any more – a pigsty. We live in a pigsty. Laugh for God's sake.

ALT: *(Wildly)* I'm laughing.

MARIE: We live in a pigsty.

ALT: We live in a pigsty.

MARIE: I was dreaming 'til now. Idiot. Idiot. In a pigsty. Laugh with me. Idiot in a pigsty. Idiot in a pigsty. Hey, I didn't hear you laugh. *(Collapses, Alt catches her and fondles her hair.)*

END OF ACT ONE

ACT TWO

Evening. Flowers in the room.

SCENE ONE

Desiree and Marie are dancing to gramophone music.

DESIREE:	Take smaller steps.
MARIE:	*(Laughs)* I haven't got it yet. Patience.
DESIREE:	You can do anything.
MARIE:	You're flirting with me too conspicuously.
DESIREE:	Marion.
MARIE:	*(Laughs)*
DESIREE:	My Marion.
MARIE:	*(Laughs)* Not yet.
DESIREE:	Don't hold your back so stiffly. The hips should be quite loose.
MARIE:	You've said it.
DESIREE:	You should take more exercise. Cold showers. Massage and Swedish gymnastics, every morning.
MARIE:	I haven't the time.
DESIREE:	We'll make the time. Exercise spares a thousand unnecessary thoughts per hour. *(Laughs)* You just trod on my foot.
MARIE:	Again.
DESIREE:	I forgive you everything.
MARIE:	Do you still love me?
DESIREE:	Silly girl.
MARIE:	*(Stops dancing.)* What was it?
DESIREE:	What?
MARIE:	*(Laughs)* It was an inner victory. 'It was an inner victory, to finally emerge from the bonds of habit.'

DESIREE: How could you learn that silly letter off by heart?

MARIE: ' – to emerge, to break away from one's self, like the prairie mustang from its locked cage.'

DESIREE: You were the cage.

MARIE: 'That little bit of prairie in us.'

DESIREE: Shut up.

MARIE: I was the cage.

DESIREE: The prairie has red hair.

MARIE: Shall I read it to you exactly? *(Searches)*

DESIREE: For God's sake. *(Winds the gramophone.)*

MARIE: *(Reads the letter.)* 'It was an inner victory to finally emerge from the bonds of habit – '

DESIREE: Listen.

MARIE: Bonds of habit.

DESIREE: This is a Javanese dance.

MARIE: Perhaps he's right.

DESIREE: Let him go. Can't you hear how beautiful it is? You can take bigger steps now.

MARIE: Like this?

DESIREE: Excellent.

MARIE: Twenty four hours ago I wouldn't have believed how quickly one forgets.

DESIREE: You've no idea how quickly.

MARIE: Or do you only imagine it?

DESIREE: *(Brutal)* If you don't concentrate you can't dance. *(Turns off the gramophone.)*

MARIE: *(Quickly)* I am concentrating.

DESIREE: You're indulging in memories.

MARIE: I was just thinking of Alt – how he broke the news to me yesterday.

DESIREE: If only Alt were a man – he'd be a God.

MARIE: He is a man.

DESIREE: *(Laughs)* You've no instinct for these things. I'd take a bath in front of him – he's like an old woman. Alt is without sex. *(Stretches herself out.)*

MARIE: But he has a child.

DESIREE: He begot the child for the sake of having a child. More difficult to imagine in a man than in a woman. Alt is a male Mummy.

MARIE: He was very strict with me yesterday.

DESIREE: He can be just as stubborn as a stupid Mama.

MARIE: He sticks his finger in your mouth so you vomit.

DESIREE: When someday I just can't manage any more.

MARIE: *(Beside her.)* You?

DESIREE: Then I'll go to him.

MARIE: You can't manage any more.

DESIREE: *(Tenderly)* Will you always stay by me?

MARIE: *(Fondles her hair.)* Darling.

DESIREE: *(Kisses her hand.)* Marion.

MARIE: *(Takes her hand away.)* No.

DESIREE: Turn off the light. Let's dream.

MARIE: *(Silent)*

DESIREE: Come on, let's go to bed.

MARIE: No, I'm not tired yet. *(Pause)* Tomorrow's my graduation party.

DESIREE: That was childish of you.

MARIE: When one wants to do something exciting, it always seems childish afterwards. – Actually it was Freder who exposed all.

DESIREE: You should thank him.

MARIE: I don't want to see him.

DESIREE: It would do you good.

MARIE: No.

DESIREE: He and Alt are like two brothers who don't look alike.

MARIE: *(Astonished)* Freder?

DESIREE: Both fight to the end without prejudice.

MARIE: Somehow I'm afraid of Freder.

DESIREE: Somehow I'm afraid of Alt. He's creepy 'cause he runs around in men's clothes.

MARIE: You see everything in a sexual context.

DESIREE: They both wear the same head on different shoulders. They've different hands, and perhaps different hearts but the same head. Man is a strange composition. You've never seen Freder when he loses control.

MARIE: Can he lose control?

DESIREE: I couldn't have put up with him for so long otherwise. He sucks your blood like a wild animal. It's not just lust, it's delirium, pain, madness. One of the few moments when we transcend the pathetic creature within. All that's left is the empty carcass.

MARIE: *(Softly)* How your face has changed.

DESIREE: *(Hugs her.)* To die Marion, to die.

MARIE: To die?

DESIREE: Just a little step beyond the fevering lust, just a little step beyond the pain – and one never wakes again. *(Kisses her passionately.)* How marvellous that would be, Marion.

MARIE: *(Sobbing, pulls Desiree to her.)* Not die. Not die.

DESIREE: We'll die together Marion. *(Sitting close together.)* Why go on? You kid yourself for a little while but you wake up again: it's the same, it's always, always the same. Why? *(Pause)* I haven't the courage. If I just whispered to Freder at that moment: bite me in the neck! Murder me! – he'd do it.

MARIE: To be murdered! I'd rather do it myself thanks.

DESIREE: It's easier to be murdered. It's more certain. I haven't the courage. I think women are clinging creatures. We even cling to the idea of consciously enjoying that final lust. – In fact I trained Freder – in case I decided. But I hadn't the courage. Two little words when he's about to go off his head. Two little words: murder me, and he'd do it. He'd bite me in the neck. He knows he's in danger.

MARIE:	Don't go on.
DESIREE:	I trained him like a wild animal. You only need to get him excited.
MARIE:	*(Looses herself from Desiree.)* No, Baby.
DESIREE:	And he'll do it sometime. Unfortunately not with me. We don't click any more.
MARIE:	Not death.
DESIREE:	*(Smiles)* Your eyes are very blue right now.
MARIE:	Don't talk.
DESIREE:	How lovely you are, Marion.
MARIE:	*(Smiles)* Let's sit quietly together.
DESIREE:	We'll sit quietly together.
MARIE:	Quietly together. Don't speak. *(Pause)*
DESIREE:	You know –
MARIE:	Yes?
DESIREE:	Just now I could –
MARIE:	Say it.
DESIREE:	*(Laughs)* Even take a look at the penny dreadful.
MARIE:	Anatomy?
DESIREE:	The paper's in three weeks.
MARIE:	Yesterday went fine –
DESIREE:	Ridiculous, others cram day and night, fail – I don't understand it.
MARIE:	I crammed day and night once.
DESIREE:	Was that difficult?
MARIE:	No, it was fun.
DESIREE:	If only easy things were fun!
MARIE:	Everybody is crazy someway.
DESIREE:	*(Helps herself from the chocolate box.)* Help yourself. *(They eat.)* Shall we dance or go to bed?
MARIE:	It's too early. We're so cosy here. I'll order tea. *(Rings)*

DESIREE: I'll go to bed and you come and sit next to me.

MARIE: Are you tired?

DESIREE: You shouldn't just go to bed when you're tired, you
            should go instead when you're in a good mood. I love
            bed. I feel safe there.

MARIE: Go on, Baby.

DESIREE: Don't leave me alone too long. *(Exits)*

MARIE: *(Looks shyly at the letter.)* ' – like the prairie mustang from
            it's locked cage – '

SCENE TWO

Lucy.

MARIE: Make us some tea, please. What's up?

LUCY: *(Smiles)* Mrs Schimmelbrot.

MARIE: Yes?

LUCY: She's not at home.

MARIE: Don't you have any tea?

LUCY: Oh yes.

MARIE: *(Offers her from the chocolates.)* Help yourself.

LUCY: Thanks. We're both from Passau.

MARIE: I didn't know.

LUCY: I saw it on the registration form.

MARIE: What were you doing with my registration form today?

LUCY: Ages ago.

MARIE: *(Watches her.)* That's nice that you're from Passau too.

LUCY: I didn't have the courage to tell you. My father worked for
            yours. My father's a carpenter.

MARIE: Why are you so happy today?

LUCY: Your father's a builder?

MARIE: Yes –

LUCY: I thought so.

MARIE:	Why are you so happy today?
LUCY:	It's so lovely outside.
MARIE:	Are you going out?
LUCY:	*(Smiles)* Perhaps.
MARIE:	Then I'll make the tea myself –
LUCY:	I can't go yet. My fiancé worked for your father as well.
MARIE:	You've got a fiancé?
LUCY:	My fiancé is a decorator.
MARIE:	Why did you leave Passau?
LUCY:	There were six of us at home.
MARIE:	Are you going to marry soon?
LUCY:	Not before I go home. That's fine that you're from Passau too.
MARIE:	*(Laughs)* Why's that fine?
LUCY:	*(Points to Desiree's door.)* I wouldn't want to come from the same town as her.
MARIE:	Ah yes.
LUCY:	But Passau is fine. All my brothers and sisters are from Passau. Now they've all gone away. *(Exits)*
MARIE:	*(Winds the gramophone and sits beside it.)*

SCENE THREE

Irene.

IRENE:	Could I have a word with you?
MARIE:	*(Silent)*
IRENE:	Just a few words.
MARIE:	*(Silent)*
IRENE:	We don't even have to sit down.
MARIE:	*(Quickly)* I beg your pardon. *(They sit down.)*
IRENE:	Perhaps you could turn the gramophone off for a bit?

MARIE:	It irritates you?
IRENE:	Whatever you like. I don't want any misunderstandings.
MARIE:	You like to be exact.
IRENE:	Mr Petrell wasn't here?
MARIE:	Now that's a lie.
IRENE:	Listen to me.
MARIE:	Petrell would never come here. He's a coward.
IRENE:	It depends on the influence.
MARIE:	*(Laughs)* Ah yes.
IRENE:	Nobody can exist alone.
MARIE:	He'll soon take courage – with your influence.
IRENE:	You're nervous.
MARIE:	You're teaching him to be a hero.
IRENE:	Do you really like this music? *(Marie silent.)* One can hardly hear oneself speak.
MARIE:	Strange that someone can become rounder in just twenty-four hours.
IRENE:	What do you mean?
MARIE:	Your face is fuller. Full and serene.
IRENE:	I've probably put on weight.
MARIE:	Suddenly your face has lost its sharpness. You're beautiful. *(Rises and turns off the gramophone.)*
IRENE:	Thank goodness.
MARIE:	Make yourself at home.
IRENE:	We want to settle everything objectively.
MARIE:	Ah yes, objectively.
IRENE:	Mr Petrell –
MARIE:	Say Otto. Mr Petrell sounds like a lie.
IRENE:	You're mistaken. We're not quite that far yet.
MARIE:	I received a letter from him this morning.
IRENE:	I know.

MARIE:	*(Looks at her.)* He shows you his letters? Perhaps you wrote it together?
IRENE:	He has his own style.
MARIE:	I know. The prairie mustang in its cage.
IRENE:	He's a poet.
MARIE:	He's a poet.
IRENE:	I wanted to offer you our friendship.
MARIE:	Thanks.
IRENE:	You've done a lot for him.
MARIE:	Thanks.
IRENE:	You helped him through very bad times.
MARIE:	*(Excited)* Thanks.
IRENE:	He'll never forget that. He talks very highly of you. You were more than a mother to him.
MARIE:	*(Beside herself.)* Be quiet for God's sake.
IRENE:	I don't understand you.
MARIE:	You don't understand me.
IRENE:	You mean a lot to him. He could never cut you out of his life.
MARIE:	The prairie mustang.
IRENE:	Those are literary clichés.
MARIE:	They could be yours. Do you write his essays for him too?
IRENE:	One can't talk to you.
MARIE:	I'm not a fish.
IRENE:	Nobody said so. *(Rises)*
MARIE:	Sit down.
IRENE:	Marie.
MARIE:	I'm not a fish.
IRENE:	Why are you not a fish?
MARIE:	Why don't you just say it – what do you want here?
IRENE:	I wanted to offer you our friendship.

MARIE:	Thanks.
IRENE:	And now my mission has ended.
MARIE:	Thanks.
IRENE:	Until you're more reasonable.
MARIE:	Sit down.
IRENE:	I don't want to disturb your evening music.
MARIE:	Sit down.
IRENE:	I've got things to do.
MARIE:	Sit down.
IRENE:	We're not playing school.
MARIE:	Sit down.
IRENE:	You seem –
MARIE:	*(Beside herself.)* Sit down.
IRENE:	What does this mean? *(Sits)*
MARIE:	*(Tears the hat from her head.)* We'll drink tea together.
IRENE:	I've things to do.
MARIE:	At the moment you're here with me.
IRENE:	*(Uncertain)* I won't let myself be bullied.
MARIE:	Thanks for the visit.
IRENE:	I like to be plain.
MARIE:	*(Offers the chocolates.)* Have one.
IRENE:	I don't like sweet things.
MARIE:	From Desiree. She gave me a present today. Nice isn't it? The flowers are also from Desiree. Take a look.
IRENE:	Very nice of her.
MARIE:	No, the box is nice.
IRENE:	What does all this mean?
MARIE:	Well then – your friendship.
IRENE:	Take your time and think it over.
MARIE:	What do you mean – your friendship?

IRENE: Just think it over. You've plenty of time.

MARIE: I'm all right – was it his idea?

IRENE: That doesn't matter.

MARIE: He doesn't say so in the letter.

IRENE: It occurred to us afterwards.

MARIE: Who?

IRENE: It goes without saying, you don't have to write it down.

MARIE: I don't find it so obvious.

IRENE: After living together two years?

MARIE: You taught him that too?

IRENE: You seem to think he's an idiot.

MARIE: He's ruthless and indifferent. The ruthlessness comes from the indifference. He's not a bad person.

IRENE: Nobody said so.

MARIE: None the less, it would never have occurred to him to offer his friendship already. That's your idea.

IRENE: It doesn't matter.

MARIE: It does matter because you're a bad person.

IRENE: If it pleases you.

MARIE: You do it to tidy up.

IRENE: *(Laughs)*

MARIE: You weigh up the emotions.

IRENE: I didn't know that.

MARIE: You taught him the exact amount of gratitude so you don't feel threatened.

IRENE: Just keep on talking. It seems to do you good.

MARIE: You do it on purpose, but without feeling. You're a fish.

IRENE: Ah yes. I'm the fish.

MARIE: You have your target.

IRENE: I don't deny it.

MARIE: Your ambition is like a machine. Ruthless and inconsiderate, straight at the target.

IRENE: I've worked enough at it.

MARIE: I know.

IRENE: I didn't get my education in bed.

MARIE: I know.

IRENE: But in a cold room.

MARIE: You starved for your ambition.

IRENE: I starved.

MARIE: Because you're proud of it.

IRENE: Of starving?

MARIE: Of starving.

IRENE: Your conclusions amaze me.

MARIE: You tell everyone you had to starve in order to study.

IRENE: Because other young women who aren't exactly ugly manage to earn their money by other means.

MARIE: No one's accusing you.

IRENE: Young people don't have to be accused. They're capable of anything. It's not enough to merely emerge from the battle of adolescence relatively unscathed; you have to win it hands down.

MARIE: *(Softly)* I don't want to win any more.

IRENE: Awakened youth, lost on life's highways, are in imminent danger of their lives. And we aimless, post war generation – youth itself becomes a sickness.

MARIE: I don't want to win.

IRENE: You'll discover yourself again.

MARIE: *(Looks at her.)*

IRENE: We survive everything we want to survive.

MARIE: You know that beforehand. *(Irene silent.)* That's why you came here?

IRENE: We could become friends.

MARIE: You need me then?

IRENE: *(Looks uncertain.)*

MARIE: You'll both stand by me?

IRENE: If you wish.

MARIE: I don't –

IRENE: Then excuse the intrusion. *(Rises)*

MARIE: I don't ever want to see either of you again.

IRENE: We'll respect that.

MARIE: I hate the whole hypocrisy.

IRENE: Don't get excited again.

MARIE: Your goodness, your eagerness – all hypocrisy. You just
            want power. Not with me.

IRENE: Let's part in peace.

MARIE: I see through you, you – you Irma you.

IRENE: Now you're being vulgar.

MARIE: You said it yourself.

IRENE: And if I am called Irma?

MARIE: You call yourself Irene. Everything about you is
            hypocritical.

IRENE: *(Goes to the door.)*

MARIE: A porter's daughter called Irene.

IRENE: Let me out.

MARIE: *(Blocks the door.)* Sit down.

IRENE: You've gone mad.

MARIE: Sit down.

IRENE: Let me out. *(Touches her.)*

MARIE: *(Pushes her.)* Sit down, Irma.

IRENE: I'll call for help.

MARIE: Call, Irma. He can't hear you downstairs.

IRENE: *(Approaches Marie.)* I won't let you stop me.

MARIE: *(Pulls her hair.)* That's the prairie, isn't it. The red prairie. Why else would you let your hair grow?

IRENE: *(Beside herself.)* Let me go, you.

MARIE: *(Laughs)* To be different. All hypocrisy.

IRENE: I'll hit you. *(They fight.)*

MARIE: *(Laughs)* He'll wait downstairs. Don't worry. He can be trained to do anything. You know that fine well, little Irmy. *(Drags Irene through the room and ties her by the hair to a cupboard leg.)* Thalatta! Thalatta! Freder's war cry. Let's play Red Indians. *(Laughs hysterically.)* Red scalp, red scalp tied to a cupboard. To a prairie cupboard. *(Jumps up.)* Let's go get the wild mustang. *(Exit)*

IRENE: *(Calls after her, wild.)* You'll do yourself in, anyway. *(Tries to undo her hair.)*

SCENE FOUR

Freder enters from Desiree's room.

FREDER: Why are you sitting on the floor?

IRENE: She'll pay dear for that.

FREDER: You seem to be tied up by your hair.

IRENE: She'll pay dear for that.

FREDER: It's not so easy to undo.

IRENE: You're hurting me.

FREDER: You have got a mass of hair.

IRENE: Let me be. I'll do it myself.

FREDER: Lovely, thick hair – what were you up to here?

IRENE: We felt sorry for her.

FREDER: Take it easy, you'll tie yourself in knots. *(Helps)*

IRENE: She's ripe to kill him.

FREDER: He's waiting downstairs?

IRENE: No, he's not downstairs.

FREDER: But somewhere near?

IRENE:	Take your hands away.
FREDER:	*(Laughs)* Only when I want. That's the way to get yourself in a pickle, little girl and suddenly it's too late. Now I can do what I want with you little witch. Ticklish?
IRENE:	*(Wild)* Let me go.
FREDER:	You've never slept with a man, what?
IRENE:	I'm just dying to tell you all about it.
FREDER:	First the altar, then bed. You're tearing it out in handfuls.
IRENE:	*(Freed) (Runs to the mirror to tidy herself.)* You'll never see me again. *(Exit)*
FREDER:	He'll get a surprise. Untidy girl. *(Goes into Desiree's room.)*

SCENE FIVE

Lucy with a tea tray.

LUCY:	*(At Desiree's door.)* Shall I bring in the tea?
FREDER:	*(Appears)* Who's it for?
LUCY:	*(Quietly)* Miss Marie ordered it.
FREDER:	Put it on the table. *(Lucy does so.)* Is that your Sunday best?
LUCY:	Yes.
FREDER:	Come here. Look at me.
LUCY:	Mr Freder.
FREDER:	Why the smile? Happy?
LUCY:	Mrs Schimmelbrot's not here.
FREDER:	Where's Mrs Schimmelbrot gone?
LUCY:	I don't know.
FREDER:	Is she often out?
LUCY:	No, seldom.
FREDER:	Then she's probably gone to a party. Did she look for the rings?

LUCY:	She still hasn't noticed.
FREDER:	She hasn't gone to a party, she's visiting poor relatives. Why are you laughing? One doesn't wear rings when visiting poor relations.
LUCY:	*(Laughs)* No.
FREDER:	Going already?
LUCY:	If you want.
FREDER:	We still have time. *(Pours tea.)* Sit down.
LUCY:	*(Laughs)*
FREDER:	Why are you laughing?
LUCY:	I'm so happy.
FREDER:	Drink up. *(Offers her the chocolates.)*
LUCY:	Miss Marie gave me one.
FREDER:	Drink and eat up. *(Goes into Desiree's room, leaving the door open.)* *(From within.)* With your permission?
DESIREE:	*(From within, laughs.)*
FREDER:	*(From within.)* For Miss Lucy.
DESIREE:	*(From within.)* What nonsense. *(Laugh)*
FREDER:	*(From within.)* Don't get up. I can find it myself.
LUCY:	*(Listens intently.)*
DESIREE:	*(From within.)* Are you going out together?
FREDER:	Yes. *(Enters)* *(Powder and make-up utensils.)* Stay seated Lucy.
LUCY:	*(Shocked)* Mr Freder.
FREDER:	Tomorrow I'll buy you your own. *(Sits opposite.)* Hold your head up.
LUCY:	*(Quietly)* I don't know how to do it.
FREDER:	I'll show you. Especially the eyes. *(Starts to make-up.)*
LUCY:	Mr Freder.
FREDER:	Why all the excitement?
LUCY:	Will it suit me?

FREDER:	Trust me.
LUCY:	Yes.
FREDER:	Hold your head still. Never had a powder puff in the hand?
LUCY:	No.
FREDER:	Natural beauty is only a base.
LUCY:	*(Ingenuous)* Yes.
FREDER:	Your face has soul in it, but it will only be attractive if I give it a precise expression. Why are you trembling? Prickly?
LUCY:	Mr Freder.
FREDER:	*(Laughs)* Excited aren't you? Want to give me a big hug?
LUCY:	*(Silent)*
FREDER:	Now the cheeks.
LUCY:	Now I know.
FREDER:	What do you know?
LUCY:	You think I'm ugly.
FREDER:	Rubbish.
LUCY:	You wouldn't paint me otherwise.
FREDER:	You're beautiful but it needs underlining.
LUCY:	*(Uncertain)* Yes.
FREDER:	Natural beauty smells of carbolic soap. Don't move the lips.
LUCY:	*(Quickly)* Mr Freder.
FREDER:	What's up?
LUCY:	You don't want to kiss me any more.
FREDER:	*(Laughs)* You're mad.
LUCY:	You'll be disgusted by the red colour.
FREDER:	Still.
LUCY:	Please, no Mr Freder.
FREDER:	*(Forcing her.)* Still girl.

Lucy:	Please, not the lips.
Freder:	Just wait and see how I'll kiss you.
Lucy:	*(Unresisting)* Mr Freder.
Freder:	Have a look in the mirror.
Lucy:	*(Lingers by the mirror.)* That's not me.
Freder:	You, at your best. Do you see how beautiful you are?
Lucy:	*(Silent)*
Freder:	I'll bring you a wonderful evening coat.
Lucy:	Please Mr Freder. Please, no.
Freder:	And a little hat.
Lucy:	*(Dizzy)* No.
Freder:	Then we'll go out together. *(Into Desy's room.)*
Lucy:	*(Sinks onto the stool.)*
Freder:	*(With Desy's hat and coat.)* Crying? Hold your head up. You're smudging the eye make-up. Here take my handkerchief.
Lucy:	*(Dries her eyes.)*
Freder:	*(Helps her into the coat.)* Now you're laughing, what?
Lucy:	*(Looks at him.)*
Freder:	Laugh.
Lucy:	*(Smiles)*
Freder:	Laugh properly. *(Kisses her on the mouth.)*
Lucy:	*(Comforted)* Mr Freder.
Freder:	My honey-mouth. Are you happy?
Lucy:	*(Laughs warmly.)* If you like me like this.
Freder:	You're beautiful.
Lucy:	And the hat. *(Puts it on.)*
Freder:	Now you're talking.
Lucy:	*(Looks in the mirror.)*
Freder:	You'll conquer hearts.
Lucy:	I'm ashamed.

FREDER: People will turn round and look at you.

LUCY: I feel so funny.

FREDER: People will talk to you.

LUCY: If you're with me, nobody'll dare.

FREDER: And if I'm not with you?

LUCY: You're going to leave me alone?

FREDER: Wouldn't that be fun?

LUCY: I'd kill myself.

FREDER: You're very fond of me.

LUCY: I'm very fond of you.

FREDER: And if I want you to let people talk to you?

LUCY: *(Confused)* I don't know what you mean.

FREDER: A nice, handsome young man?

LUCY: No, Mr Freder.

FREDER: Just look in the mirror. A nice, rich young man could fall for you.

LUCY: What do I care.

FREDER: You just love me, don't you?

LUCY: Are we going to a fancy-dress? I've never been to a fancy-dress ball.

FREDER: And you feel all dressed up.

LUCY: *(Laughs)* Especially the face.

DESIREE: *(Appears at the door.)* Let's have a look at you, Miss Lucy.

LUCY: *(Shocked)* My God! *(Exits)*

DESIREE: She looks a sight.

FREDER: *(Laughs)* She's ashamed.

DESIREE: Is she going to walk the streets?

FREDER: Very many thanks. *(Exits)*

SCENE SIX

Marie and Petrell.

MARIE: Come on. *(To Desiree.)* Leave us alone.

DESIREE: *(Goes)*

MARIE: *(Forces him in.)* She's not here any more. She waited so nicely for you. She got bored. *(Laughs)*

PETRELL: Where is Irene?

MARIE: She got bored. Why don't you sit down – I won't bite.

PETRELL: *(Stays put.)* What do you want?

MARIE: Not you any more. Don't be afraid.

PETRELL: What do you want?

MARIE: I'd rather run the streets like some stupid cow. Sit down.

PETRELL: When you've calmed down.

MARIE: I'm calm now.

PETRELL: I know you too well.

MARIE: Thanks.

PETRELL: Why do we have to part like this?

MARIE: Keep the soft tones for her.

PETRELL: I want to explain to you.

MARIE: If I wanted you'd be back like a shot. You've no backbone.

PETRELL: You don't want to be reasonable.

MARIE: Why don't I want to be reasonable?

PETRELL: You don't talk.

MARIE: Perhaps I sing?

PETRELL: You screech.

MARIE: *(Laughs)* I screech.

PETRELL: Metaphorically speaking.

MARIE: And she flutes.

PETRELL: Oh, be quiet.

MARIE: And I screech.

PETRELL: I didn't say, you screech.

MARIE: You said that I screech.

PETRELL: I meant that you're over-excited.

MARIE: You said that I screech.

PETRELL: Too excited to be reasonable.

MARIE: You said that I screech.

PETRELL: If you insist.

MARIE: Who said I insist?

PETRELL: Why did you drag me here?

MARIE: To collect Irene.

PETRELL: You're lying.

MARIE: To go home with her.

PETRELL: She was gone and you ran after her.

MARIE: She wasn't gone. *(Laughs)*

PETRELL: She would have stopped you attacking me.

MARIE: *(Laughs)* It's difficult to stop sometimes.

PETRELL: You ran after her and stopped her.

MARIE: You're no good at reconstruction. Take a look, maybe
            you'll find a little bit of her in this room.

PETRELL: Let's meet some other time.

MARIE: A little bit of prairie, right here.

PETRELL: When you've quietened down.

MARIE: Go find, mustang, go find.

PETRELL: I've had enough. *(Attempts to go.)*

MARIE: Go find, mustang. Prairie, red prairie. Cold. Cold.
            (Laughs) Go to the cupboard, it's warmer there. Warm.
            (Pushes him to the cupboard.) Open your eyes. Don't you
            see anything? *(Triumphant)* Here's the prairie.
            (Displaying a few of Irene's hairs.)

PETRELL: *(Shocked)* What have you done to her?

MARIE: We played cowboys and indians.

PETRELL: *(Horrified)* Marie.

MARIE: *(Laughing loudly.)* Played indians. Like you said in your letter, mustang. I scalped her. Scalped chief redskin.

PETRELL: *(Grabs her, horrified.)* Marie.

MARIE: *(Suddenly motionless, looks at him.)*

PETRELL: *(Softly)* What did you do to her?

MARIE: *(Looks astonished.)*

PETRELL: Did you –

MARIE: *(Softly)* Let me go.

PETRELL: Have you gone mad?

MARIE: Don't touch me again.

PETRELL: I want to know what you've done to her.

MARIE: Nothing.

PETRELL: *(Violently)* Where is Irene?

MARIE: *(Suddenly)* What if I murdered her?

PETRELL: I don't believe you any more.

MARIE: I murdered her.

PETRELL: I don't believe you any more.

MARIE: And just now you were scared silly.

PETRELL: But I don't believe you any more.

MARIE: But you were scared.

PETRELL: I don't believe you would do it.

MARIE: You could be mistaken.

PETRELL: I can see it in your eyes.

MARIE: Percipient.

PETRELL: Where is Irene?

MARIE: In the kitchen. The police will be here in a minute. The doctor's there too.

PETRELL: You've hidden her.

MARIE: Ask the doctor. I strangled her. If you stay you may be arrested too.

PETRELL: You've locked her up. Is she in Desiree's room?

MARIE: I wouldn't ask too many questions if I were you. I'd have a look in the kitchen or are you afraid?

PETRELL: You enjoy seeing me suffer.

MARIE: *(Changes her mind.)* She's unharmed.

PETRELL: Where is she then?

MARIE: At home.

PETRELL: At home?

MARIE: Or at your place. Do you love her so very much?

PETRELL: Did you leave together?

MARIE: *(Exhausted)* I tied her up so she wouldn't stop me. She'll be very useful. You'll go places. She's very clever.

PETRELL: *(Amazed)* By the hair?

MARIE: *(Nods)* Tell me, when did you first fall in love with her?

PETRELL: You've gone mad.

MARIE: Forgive me. Do you love her very much?

PETRELL: Let me be.

MARIE: You're hurt. Can't you forgive me?

PETRELL: I'm going now.

MARIE: Won't you forgive me? Kiss me.

PETRELL: I have to go now.

MARIE: Hate. Hate forever? With her assistance you'll be famous.

PETRELL: I knew it was a mistake from the very beginning.

MARIE: What was a mistake?

PETRELL: All the best.

MARIE: That you both came here? That was a mistake. You know me better than she does. She shouldn't have talked you into it. Say something, answer.

PETRELL: I still wouldn't have imagined you could be so mean.

MARIE: She'll have a great career. You'll both have great careers.

PETRELL: *(Attempts to leave.)*

MARIE: *(Suddenly)* Hit me then.

PETRELL: You're out of your mind.

MARIE: Hit me, if you can't forgive me.

PETRELL: Do you want the entire house to hear.

MARIE: You despise me.

PETRELL: Shouting won't get us any further.

MARIE: Hit me then.

PETRELL: Stop screaming.

MARIE: What can I do so you'll hit me? I hit her too. I tied her up by the hair. I tied her up like a mangy dog. *(Screaming)* Go ahead, hit me.

PETRELL: *(Attempts to reach the door.)*

MARIE: Stay put. You don't take to your heels like that, after loving a woman two long years. Or was that a lie?

PETRELL: I can't stand it. *(Opens the door.)*

MARIE: *(Violent)* And my money?

PETRELL: Your money?

MARIE: My money. Or didn't you live off me?

PETRELL: *(Closes the door.)* Do you want the whole house to hear?

MARIE: The whole house can hear that I've been keeping you for two years.

PETRELL: *(Pale)* Have you lost your senses?

MARIE: That took your breath away. Who took everything I bought him? And who worked night and day, to buy him his meals? And who took the suits and books and shoes and shirts and socks I bought him?

PETRELL: I'll pay every penny back.

MARIE: Go on, leave me high and dry. She keeps every penny for herself.

PETRELL: I earn money.

MARIE: And who got blisters on her feet running around to find you work?

PETRELL: I'm not denying it.

MARIE: And sent you to a sanatorium for your lungs which was a cock and bull story.

PETRELL: The situation is getting embarrassing.

MARIE: He's embarrassed.

PETRELL: It's the cross-examination of a thief.

MARIE: You're not a thief?

PETRELL: Marie.

MARIE: Are you a thief?

PETRELL: You don't know what you're saying any more.

MARIE: You are a thief.

PETRELL: I've had enough. *(Goes to the door.)*

MARIE: Hit me then if you're not a thief.

PETRELL: The entire building can hear for all I care.

MARIE: Hit me then. *(Holds him.)* Hit me if you're not a thief. Have you no pity?

PETRELL: You need a cold bath.

MARIE: *(Falls to her knees, crying.)* Hit me if you're not a thief.

PETRELL: This madness is infectious. *(Tears himself away.)*

MARIE: I won't let you go until you hit me. I won't let you go.

PETRELL: You belong in the madhouse. *(Exits)*

MARIE: Hit me, hit me, hit me.

SCENE SEVEN

Desiree enters.

DESIREE: *(Kneels beside her.)* Marion.

MARIE: *(Smiling)* Hit me. You're not a thief.

DESIREE: *(Helps her up.)* Poor little girl.

MARIE: He didn't hit me.

DESIREE: Come. I'll kiss your tears away.

MARIE: Yes, kiss me.

DESIREE: My little Marion.

MARIE: He didn't hit me. Kiss me again.

DESIREE: *(Kisses her passionately.)* Let's go and lie down together in my nice warm bed, and warm ourselves up.

MARIE: Very close together.

DESIREE: Warm, like a couple of kids. I'll tell you a story, Marion, like two little girls at bedtime.

MARIE: Like two little girls at bedtime. Lights out, little girls.

DESIREE: All mine. *(Exit both, embracing.)*

END OF ACT TWO

ACT THREE

SCENE ONE

Evening. Marie, Desiree, Alt, Freder.

FREDER: *(Stretched out.)* My liver's playing up.

ALT: Drink less.

FREDER: My liver's gone to my head.

DESIREE: You'll collapse sometime.

FREDER: I sleep with my knees in my stomach.

DESIREE: *(Laughs)* For God's sake!

FREDER: It's not so painful.

DESIREE: It's time you married.

FREDER: How about it, Marie?

MARIE: *(Laughs)* Idiot.

DESIREE: He's seriously offering.

FREDER: Very serious. We'd be the perfect pair.

DESIREE: She'll think about it. She's beginning to appreciate you.

FREDER: I'll improve.

DESIREE: He'll improve.

FREDER: Some more water.

DESIREE: Why don't you answer him?

FREDER: *(Rises)* Quite consciously choose the right moment and become a solid citizen.

DESIREE: Bravo. He has realistic intentions.

MARIE: *(Looks at her.)*

DESIREE: His liver has made him sensible. I'm not laughing.

FREDER: *(Writhes)* Painful.

DESIREE: Don't look at me like that, Marion.

ALT: What is pain? *(Stretches out.)*

FREDER: *(To Marie.)* Think about it.

MARIE: Leave me alone.

FREDER: I need to be cared for. I don't like work. You love it. We're an excellent pair. We've become so close, the marriage is only a formality.

MARIE: Freder believes in form.

FREDER: I promise to break all ties with Lucy the moment you decide.

DESIREE: Have you ties with Lucy?

FREDER: She far outreaches all expectation.

MARIE: Marry Lucy.

FREDER: I'm not a pimp.

DESIREE: You misunderstand him.

MARIE: Do you enjoy that?

DESIREE: Either you become a solid citizen or you kill yourself. There's no other alternative, I'm not joking.

FREDER: *(To Marie.)* We've already kissed.

MARIE: *(Laughs)* You're both not right in the head.

FREDER: Do you deny it?

DESIREE: When did you kiss?

FREDER: Yesterday evening.

MARIE: You were there.

DESIREE: I don't remember.

MARIE: It was your idea.

DESIREE: You're dreaming.

MARIE: You wouldn't leave us alone, Desy. Finally, I kissed him.

DESIREE: I've completely forgotten.

MARIE: You were so drunk.

FREDER: It hurts every time I breathe God in heaven!

DESIREE: Not so loud. Alt's sleeping.

ALT: Pain isn't an organic change in the body. The wounded soldier still runs on as if nothing had happened.

DESIREE: I feel pain when somebody stands on my little toe.

ALT: And when tuberculosis germs eat your lungs away you don't feel a thing. Pain is self-indulgent.

MARIE: I often stood on your little toe.

DESIREE: I don't dance with you any more.

MARIE: *(Laughs)* She's had enough of me.

DESIREE: Answer Freder.

ALT: An impulse, a psychological state of mind, self-suggestion with a subtle break, the scream.

FREDER: I must take a hot footbath. *(Exits)*

MARIE: *(Quietly)* You've had enough of me?

DESIREE: *(Silent)*

MARIE: You can tell me.

ALT: Our most sensitive nerves exist between the poles, pain and sleep. We love them both. Both, even absolute nothingness, satisfies our very existence.

DESIREE: I've a good trick to combine the poles.

ALT: *(Looks at her.)*

DESIREE: Pain and sleep together. Go on, Alt. Tea please.

MARIE: *(Pours)*

DESIREE: Sugar and cognac. *(To Alt.)* Don't wrack your brains.

ALT: I'm not wracking my brains.

DESIREE: Have you guessed?

MARIE: What should he guess?

DESIREE: Quiet baby. Just think about your Poet.

MARIE: Him.

DESIREE: If you don't do something soon, they'll marry.

MARIE: I'll propose the toast myself!

DESIREE: He'll be there until death they depart. He'll adore her male protest even when she's a granny. Hurry up, Marion.

MARIE: Are you going to leave me?

DESIREE:	You're a clinging creature. I'm planning your future.
MARIE:	I'll manage fine without you.
DESIREE:	There's still Freder's offer.
MARIE:	*(Hugs her.)* She's very quarrelsome, these last few days.
DESIREE:	*(Escapes)* Let go.
MARIE:	It's only a passing phase.
DESIREE:	Marital scenes. Some women can only think in terms of marriage, even with another woman.
MARIE:	Why are you in such a bad mood?
DESIREE:	I now know why little boy couldn't stand it any more.
MARIE:	*(Quietly)* You –
DESIREE:	It gets worse and worse. You must get a grip on yourself.
MARIE:	Won't you give me a kiss?
DESIREE:	No I won't kiss you. Go and sit down.
MARIE:	*(Sits)*
DESIREE:	She reminds me of the business man from Hamburg who wanted to marry me at all costs. Handsome young man. Nearly fainted when I gave him a kiss once. Even with prostitutes, he played husbands and wives. Talked to them about his mother, about business and even about the possibility of an improvement in the political situation in Germany in the near future.
MARIE:	I'm going to get a grey mouliné coat made, wrap-around form.
DESIREE:	You've a fitting for the jacket, tomorrow.
MARIE:	Tomorrow afternoon.
DESIREE:	I'll go with you. He shouldn't cut the vest too low.
MARIE:	You show him.
ALT:	Where did you get your pyjamas? You both look amazing.
DESIREE:	Especially Marion. *(Tenderly)* You're a sight for sore eyes in blue. I chose this blue myself. It suits your hair. *(Kisses her.)*
MARIE:	Friends again.

DESIREE:	She always establishes facts.
MARIE:	I won't do it again.
DESIREE:	It's awful.
MARIE:	Awful?
DESIREE:	Registering, making conclusions, habit. Marital existence. Suffocation.
ALT:	Out with it. What's up?
DESIREE:	Go easy.
ALT:	I'll stick my finger down your throat.
DESIREE:	Thanks.
ALT:	You need to get things off your chest, let your soul go to the toilet.
DESIREE:	Now it's my turn.
ALT:	*(Vehement)* You don't desert.
DESIREE:	I don't care about moral principles.
ALT:	It's not a moral principle. It's our only duty to man in society.
DESIREE:	Now you're getting sentimental.
ALT:	You can do what you like with yourself. But the basis for existence and the only possibility of denying its absurdity is to live your life to the end. Murder somebody else, not yourself. Murdering yourself endangers all others.
DESIREE:	That's the first time I've heard you talk clichés.
MARIE:	It isn't cliché – the only feeling of divinity we possess.
ALT:	Bravo. Take your cocaine.
DESIREE:	We don't understand each other, this time. Freder understands me better.
ALT:	Freder would never kill himself.
DESIREE:	He likes life. But he wouldn't stop anyone else.
ALT:	Not cocaine – veronal. A nice big dose of veronal. You go to sleep slowly, lose yourself in the depths – and finally, it's over.

MARIE:	I'm still a stranger.
DESIREE:	Little Marion.
MARIE:	You only get ideas like that when you're indifferent to everyone.
DESIREE:	*(Tenderly)* Don't be sad, Marion.
MARIE:	*(Smiles)* I'm just establishing facts again.
DESIREE:	Don't be sad.
MARIE:	I'm still a stranger to you?
DESIREE:	We're probably strangers all our lives.
MARIE:	You're not a stranger to me.
DESIREE:	We've different characters. Nobody's a stranger to you. To me they're all strangers. We tried, didn't we sweetheart!
ALT:	You didn't try long enough.
DESIREE:	How long do you have to keep trying? She doesn't fit. To discover that, I didn't have to sleep with her every night.
MARIE:	*(Softly)* You take the magic out of everything.
DESIREE:	Perhaps there's a seed of reluctance in every magic – you don't fit Marion.
MARIE:	*(Nods)* I don't fit.
DESIREE:	She does everything I tell her, but it's no good.
MARIE:	I don't fit.
DESIREE:	When I picked you off the floor that evening, I felt I had you. But the pain made you relax, not me.
MARIE:	Be quiet.
DESIREE:	She's embarrassed. Alt isn't a man, he's an incomplete woman, you can undress while he's here – even the next day I found us rather amusing.
MARIE:	For God's sake be quiet –
DESIREE:	I took patience with you. I wouldn't have had that much patience with a man.
MARIE:	I can't help not having an Adam's apple.
DESIREE:	You're my little clown.

MARIE:	In my childhood, I played with dolls not swords and horses.
DESIREE:	*(Hugs her knees.)* My naive little lover.
MARIE:	*(Softly)* I need the illusion of a man.
DESIREE:	Are you unhappy?
MARIE:	*(Yes)* Yes.
DESIREE:	She's disappointed in me too.
MARIE:	Yes.
DESIREE:	*(Kisses her.)* We're two poor devils.

They embrace, pause.

What'll become of us? In two years I'll be a doctor, like you. Is that the ideal? What do you dream about?

MARIE:	I don't dream any more.
DESIREE:	Assistant doctor in the general hospital? The smell of iodine and carbolic acid. That smell your whole life long.
MARIE:	Seemed like music to me, once.
DESIREE:	The most repulsive operations on dirty unwashed strangers for ever and ever – Amen.
MARIE:	It seemed like music to be once, soothing the pains of thousands.
DESIREE:	I never believed in my fellow man. Clumsy to forget yourself for others. Even when you help them they'd rather be alone.

SCENE TWO

Enter Lucy, very dressed up.

LUCY:	*(Very merry.)* Will you be needing anything else?
DESIREE:	What's up with you?
LUCY:	Will you be needing anything else?
MARIE:	Are you going out?
LUCY:	*(Nods)* I have to.
DESIREE:	Alone?

LUCY:	*(Smiles)* I'm never alone for long.
DESIREE:	Who doesn't leave you alone?
LUCY:	I don't care who it is.
DESIREE:	Come and sit with us.
LUCY:	It's getting late.
DESIREE:	We're feeling very sad here. Make us feel merry.
LUCY:	I'm never sad.
DESIREE:	You're such a funny creature.
LUCY:	Lovely. Lovely, life is lovely.
DESIREE:	What a beautiful voice you have.
LUCY:	*(Suddenly)* I'll be right back. *(Exits)*
DESIREE:	Poor creature. How I envy her.
MARIE:	How does he do it?
ALT:	Freder?
MARIE:	*(Nods)* Not to have to think of yourself any more. Your will power taken away, and be cared for, and not to have to exist for yourself.
DESIREE:	You'd never go on the streets.
MARIE:	But to be saved from one's self?
DESIREE:	I could do the same without losing my will power, without Freder, voluntarily.

SCENE THREE

Lucy with wine and glasses.

DESIREE:	We already have the cognac.
LUCY:	This is good wine.
ALT:	Where did you get the wine?
LUCY:	I can fetch another bottle.
DESIREE:	I could kiss you.
LUCY:	I'd like to drink your health.

MARIE: We girls from Passau. *(Laughs)*

LUCY: *(Laughs)* I've forgotten Passau entirely.

MARIE: And your fiancé?

LUCY: My fiancé?

DESIREE: You have a fiancé?

MARIE: In Passau.

DESIREE: She has a fiancé in Passau.

LUCY: Go on, laugh Miss.

DESIREE: Say Desiree.

LUCY: *(Laughs)* I don't hate you any more.

DESIREE: *(Astonished)* You hated me?

LUCY: Very much.

DESIREE: Why?

LUCY: *(Silent)*

MARIE: I'm feeling miserable.

ALT: Lie down beside me.

DESIREE: Not any more?

LUCY: Don't be angry. You're so beautiful, Miss.

DESIREE: Say Desiree.

LUCY: I don't understand Mr Freder.

DESIREE: What don't you understand?

LUCY: That he doesn't love you any more.

DESIREE: But you're glad?

LUCY: I'm very happy.

DESIREE: Do you love him very much?

LUCY: I couldn't love anyone more.

DESIREE: That's lovely. Give me a kiss. *(Embraces her.)*

ALT: For all her experience she's still a child.

LUCY: The only thing that's missing now's music. We're just talking.

DESIREE:	*(Winds the gramophone.)* Let's dance.
LUCY:	The doctor doesn't dance.
DESIREE:	When does Freder come?
LUCY:	I go alone, he trusts me.
DESIREE:	Does he take the money from you?
LUCY:	Not a penny. And it's all his doing.
DESIREE:	Do you earn much money? Go on, tell.
LUCY:	It depends.
DESIREE:	Go on, tell.
LUCY:	I've even had an offer of marriage.
DESIREE:	You wouldn't consider it?
LUCY:	He can wait for ever.
DESIREE:	You must get yourself a little apartment.
LUCY:	*(Quickly)* No.
DESIREE:	Mrs Schimmelbrot will catch you.
LUCY:	I'm not afraid.
DESIREE:	Now I know. Because Freder lives here?
LUCY:	*(Quickly)* Be quiet.
DESIREE:	I won't give the game away if you tell me everything. Who lent you coat and make-up that evening?
LUCY:	*(Laughs)* I was so scared then.
DESIREE:	And it went just fine didn't it?
LUCY:	It happened very quickly.
DESIREE:	Go on, tell.
LUCY:	It's much easier than you think, Miss.
DESIREE:	Say Desiree.
LUCY:	I'm only on first names with them.
DESIREE:	Do you know very many?
LUCY:	I couldn't count them.
DESIREE:	Do I have to drag it out of you? How old are you?

LUCY:	Eighteen.
DESIREE:	That's good. You go with them all?
LUCY:	Yes.
DESIREE:	It doesn't matter what he looks like?
LUCY:	I don't even look at them.
DESIREE:	Wonderful. Nothing can happen anyway.
LUCY:	You can't make a baby that way.
DESIREE:	Why can't you make a baby that way?
LUCY:	Mr Freder said so.
DESIREE:	Do you ask a lot?
LUCY:	Yesterday I pinched the wallet while one was sleeping. I wanted to know who he was.
DESIREE:	Wonderful. Who was he?
LUCY:	*(Laughs)* A boxer.
DESIREE:	*(Suddenly)* I'll go a bit of the way with you.
LUCY:	*(Afraid)* Then nobody'll talk to me.
DESIREE:	I'll put on make-up, like you.
LUCY:	But we shouldn't go together.
DESIREE:	Don't be afraid, some men like it with two.
LUCY:	I don't know about that.
DESIREE:	You don't know about a lot of things. Wait a minute. I'll get ready quickly.
MARIE:	You're going to change?
DESIREE:	*(Laughs)* I'm going with her.
MARIE:	Have you gone crazy?
DESIREE:	Why was I ever sane?
ALT:	Come with me, Miss Lucy.
DESIREE:	I won't let you keep me back. *(Laughs)*
MARIE:	Then you'll have to fight.
DESIREE:	I want to walk the streets.

MARIE:	Desy.
DESIREE:	*(Imitates)* Desy. I want to walk the streets. *(Goes into her room.)*
LUCY:	*(Astonished)* Walk the streets?
ALT:	Come.
LUCY:	I don't walk the streets.
ALT:	Certainly not.
LUCY:	I won't let myself be insulted.
ALT:	Bravo.
LUCY:	Mr Freder'll soon teach her.
ALT:	Complain to him.
LUCY:	He jilted her.

Marie goes into Desy's room.

ALT:	She'll never get over it. Come with me, quick.
LUCY:	But you'll just bring me to the corner, Doctor?
ALT:	Have no fear. *(Exit, both.)*

SCENE FOUR

MARIE:	*(In the next room.)* Be reasonable.
DESIREE:	*(In the next room.)* Give me the key.
MARIE:	*(In the next room.)* I won't allow it.
DESIREE:	*(Enters and runs to the front door.)* Don't you dare.
MARIE:	*(After her, gets there first.)* No.
DESIREE:	You won't let me pass?
MARIE:	Desy –
DESIREE:	I'll scratch your eyes out.
MARIE:	Do what you like.
DESIREE:	You're not my mother.
MARIE:	I'm not your mother.

DESIREE: *(Jumps on her.)*

MARIE: *(Pushes her away.)* You'll have to kill me first.

DESIREE: I wouldn't do you the favour.

MARIE: Desy.

DESIREE: I want to be a whore.

MARIE: I know.

DESIREE: You've no right —

MARIE: I've no right.

DESIREE: You're mad, not me.

MARIE: I'm mad, not you.

DESIREE: Let me pass — I couldn't spend a night with you again.

MARIE: We'll sleep apart. I'll make my bed up here.

DESIREE: You bore me. You disgust me.

MARIE: You wanted it this way.

DESIREE: Tonight I desire the unknown, the dirtiest men. I want a boxer. Let me walk the streets. Are you jealous?

MARIE: Perhaps I'm jealous.

DESIREE: You've gone mad.

MARIE: Perhaps I'm mad.

DESIREE: You, husband you.

    Pause.

MARIE: *(Tenderly)* Desy.

DESIREE: *(Silent)*

MARIE: *(Sits down beside her.)* Little wild animal.

DESIREE: Give me the key.

MARIE: No.

DESIREE: Nobody ever dared to lock me in. Any man who does that is sure to be cuckolded.

MARIE: Cuckold me. Sweetheart, I didn't know how angry you can get.

DESIREE: *(Goes into her room.)*

MARIE:	*(Sitting, drinks. Goes into Desy's room.)*
DESIREE:	*(In the next room.)* Leave me alone.
MARIE:	*(In the next room.)* I won't touch you.
DESIREE:	*(In the next room.)* Give me back the key.
MARIE:	*(Laughs, enters with blanket and pillow. She makes a bed on the sofa, drinks often.)*

SCENE FIVE

Alt.

MARIE:	She's in her room.
ALT:	Calmed down?
MARIE:	On the contrary.
ALT:	We'll try tomorrow.
MARIE:	Do you want another drink?
ALT:	No thanks. Goodnight.
MARIE:	Alt?
ALT:	Yes?
MARIE:	*(Pause)* How far did you go with Lucy?
ALT:	Immediately we got downstairs, she ran away.
MARIE:	She's very attractive – Alt –
ALT:	Yes?
MARIE:	*(Pause)* Goodnight.
ALT:	You want to say something?
MARIE:	I shouldn't have stopped her.
ALT:	Rubbish.
MARIE:	I'll tell her she can go if she wants.
ALT:	Calm down. She'll sleep it off.
MARIE:	She'll not sleep the whole night.
ALT:	Let her think it over.

MARIE: She feels she's a victim.

ALT: It keeps her alive.

MARIE: *(Pause)* One shouldn't desert.

ALT: *(Emphatically)* You should never desert.

MARIE: Don't shout at me.

ALT: *(Suddenly)* I'll sleep here tonight.

MARIE: *(Laughs)*

ALT: I don't like the look of you both.

MARIE: Don't you trust me either?

ALT: Even less.

MARIE: *(Astonished)* Alt?

ALT: She usually gets over her depressions.

MARIE: I don't.

ALT: You don't. She knows already – everything disappoints.

MARIE: I don't.

ALT: You don't.

MARIE: You're always talking about her.

ALT: You –

MARIE: Yes?

ALT: You're all bunged up. You need to let go.

MARIE: Give me the instructions.

ALT: Be a bit more frivolous. Treat people badly. Forget and discover yourself again.

MARIE: Amen.

ALT: A male protest.

MARIE: Keep your ten commandments to yourself.

ALT: There were only four.

MARIE: You can't bear contradiction. You like to rule the roost with your goodness – like Freder.

ALT: Freder?

MARIE:	Desy's right. Two brothers who bear no outward resemblance. Go to bed.
ALT:	Desiree's psychology –
MARIE:	She's more instinct than we do.
ALT:	Fall in love with her again. Beg her pardon.
MARIE:	*(Looks at him.)* I'll say I'm sorry.
ALT:	From this very moment you're her slave.
MARIE:	*(Smiles)* Perhaps.
ALT:	She'll treat you badly.
MARIE:	She's always treated me badly, don't worry.
ALT:	As you wish.
MARIE:	Go to bed. Freder's here.
ALT:	I don't trust him.
MARIE:	We don't need a watchdog.
ALT:	Goodnight.
MARIE:	*(Quickly)* Alt?
ALT:	Yes?
MARIE:	*(Pause)* Goodnight. *(Exit Alt.)* *(At Desiree's door.)* Open up, stupid child – Are you already in bed? – Here's the key. I don't want to stand in your way. If you feel you have to go, then go. – Please answer. I'll leave the key here, in front of the door – you only need to open a crack. *(Pause, softly.)* Forgive me, Desy. I was afraid for you. Answer. *(Angry)* I'm not even worth answering? *(Bangs on the door.)* I'm not going to move from this spot. I'll stay in front of the door the whole night, if you don't open.

SCENE SIX

Desiree in her nightdress.

DESIREE:	*(In Marie's arms.)* Kiss me.
MARIE:	You. *(Kisses her.)*
DESIREE:	*(Very tender.)* Forgive me, Marion.

MARIE: You. *(Sitting close.)*

DESIREE: *(Smiles)* Let's die together.

MARIE: Not die.

DESIREE: Help me, Marion.

MARIE: *(Crying)* Not die.

DESIREE: I have to, little sister.

MARIE: *(Kisses her.)* I'll stay with you.

DESIREE: Let's die together. I've known it all.

MARIE: You never know everything.

DESIREE: It's as if I was under narcotics. The mask on my face. My arms are round you. But it's very foggy.

MARIE: I'll carry you into bed.

DESIREE: Such a small step.

MARIE: Don't talk.

DESIREE: I'm already halfway there. Just a little step. Do it, Marion. Give me the veronal in a glass.

MARIE: *(Begs)* Don't talk about it any more. *(Falls on her knees.)* Desy.

DESIREE: Help me, mother, help me.

MARIE: *(Unnerved)* Not another word. I implore you.

DESIREE: *(More awake.)* Would you do it? I'm quite prepared. I dreamt about you in bed.

MARIE: We'll sit close together. Don't talk.

DESIREE: How silly to want to go with the whores.

MARIE: It wasn't silly.

DESIREE: Thanks for holding me back.

MARIE: *(Imploring)* We'll go together. I'll go with you.

DESIREE: I don't need to go to the whores any more. *(Smiles)* I don't need the boxer any more. Marion, stay with me. *(Kisses her.)* I dreamt you'd help me.

MARIE·   Don't talk about it any more.

DESIREE:	You called me. You banged on the door and wakened me. Say you'll do it. Say yes even if you wouldn't.
MARIE:	Why do you torture me?
DESIREE:	Just say yes, it comforts me.
MARIE:	*(Softly)* Yes.
DESIREE:	Thank you.
MARIE:	I'm going to carry you to bed.
DESIREE:	Look at me.
MARIE:	*(Lifts her in her arms.)* Come.
DESIREE:	Beautiful, strong eyes.
MARIE:	*(Carrying her.)* You'll sleep well.
DESIREE:	You're beautiful, Marion. *(Hugs her.)* Forgive me.
MARIE:	*(Carrying her.)* I'll sit beside you 'til you've gone to sleep. *(From the next room.)* Are you comfortable?
DESIREE:	*(From the next room.)* I love you, Marion.
MARIE:	*(From the next room.)* I'll turn out the light. *(The room offstage darkens.)* Go to sleep, sweetheart.
DESIREE:	*(From the next room.)* I love you.
MARIE:	*(After a while.)* Are you asleep? *(Silence)*

SCENE SEVEN

Freder, without a coat.

FREDER:	*(At Desy's door.)* Asleep at this hour?
MARIE:	*(Enters, closing the door.)* She's sleeping.
FREDER:	Are you tired too?
MARIE:	Yes.
FREDER:	At this hour? *(Pours wine.)*
MARIE:	Stop drinking.
FREDER:	We're not married yet.
MARIE:	Nonsense.

FREDER: How long will it be just nonsense?

MARIE: You're confusing me with Lucy.

FREDER: Lucy's ingenuous.

MARIE: So I see.

FREDER: She achieves things with the surety of a sleepwalker.
            I envy her.

MARIE: She's come a long way. How do you do it?

FREDER: She does it herself. Not me.

MARIE: You know what I mean.

FREDER: I've never seen you look so well.

MARIE: Stop drinking.

FREDER: One more glass won't make any difference. The footbath
            did me good. I'm ready for anything.

MARIE: Leave me alone.

FREDER: I can't sleep yet.

MARIE: But I'm tired.

FREDER: You're not very considerate.

MARIE: *(Exhausted)* Have some pity.

FREDER: I've never seen you so beautiful.

MARIE: I can't stand up any more.

FREDER: You're so pale you make me crazy.

MARIE: I feel awful.

FREDER: Exactly.

MARIE: I'm worried about Desy.

FREDER: What's wrong with Desy?

MARIE: She wanted to go with Lucy. I held her back. I shouldn't
            have done it.

FREDER: Desy's not made for it. She's too much will power and too
            little resistance. A very unlucky mixture.

MARIE: I'm worried about her.

FREDER: It leads to suicide.

MARIE:	Shut up. You took her resistance away.
FREDER:	By running away at seventeen? I only accelerated the unavoidable.
MARIE:	I wish she'd never met you.
FREDER:	*(Laughs)* You all need me.
MARIE:	You're round the bend.
FREDER:	You desire me too.
MARIE:	No answer.
FREDER:	Like the knife. *(Approaches)*
MARIE:	Leave me alone.
FREDER:	You smell blood. There's only one answer – we'll marry.
MARIE:	*(Laughs)* A fine way out.
FREDER:	Our last chance before the catastrophe. Become solid citizens.
MARIE:	Desiree's words.
FREDER:	She's more intelligent than you.
MARIE:	Perhaps.
FREDER:	She has a wider perspective. You should live on your nerves. You're totally unconscious, like Lucy.
MARIE:	We're both from Passau.
FREDER:	What?
MARIE:	I just remembered.
FREDER:	I could force you like I forced Lucy. You just need putting on the right tracks, it doesn't matter which.
MARIE:	You're joking. Are you quite finished?
FREDER:	You have so much. You could work like a dog twenty hours in the operating theatre. You could be a mother of ten. You could be the most tenacious whore. You're the perfect model of youth itself. You little Sunday's child.
MARIE:	I must try sometime.
FREDER:	But you couldn't manage being a nobody. That would be the absolute end.

MARIE:	I'll consider it.
FREDER:	I'm not joking. Take up a moral career and you'll prove to be the most gorgeous specimen of humanity.
MARIE:	I'll consider that too.
FREDER:	I'm not joking.
MARIE:	You don't impress me.
FREDER:	I only want to help you.
MARIE:	Help Lucy.
FREDER:	She doesn't need me any more. She only needed wakening.
MARIE:	Let me sleep.
FREDER:	You don't want to.
MARIE:	Who says?
FREDER:	I'm not thick skinned. You want to wake up. But with little boy it was nice to stay in bed.
MARIE:	Leave him out of it.
FREDER:	Now you have to search. It will do you good. Come out of hibernation too late and you die.
MARIE:	Will you please leave me alone.
FREDER:	Seriously, the offer still stands.
MARIE:	I'm married already.
FREDER:	To Desy?
MARIE:	To Desy.
FREDER:	You'll soon be a widow.
MARIE:	I hate you. *(Jumps up.)*
FREDER:	Finally.
MARIE:	I despise you.
FREDER:	That's love.
MARIE:	I could kill you.
FREDER:	Bravo. Thalatta! Thalatta!
MARIE:	*(Wildly)* You haven't caught me yet.

FREDER:	Do you give up?
MARIE:	You don't know me.
FREDER:	I already have you.
MARIE:	You don't dare.
FREDER:	Without touching, I've got you in my hands.
MARIE:	You're dreaming.
FREDER:	We'll both dream.
MARIE:	I'd rather kill myself.
FREDER:	You despise me that much?
MARIE:	I detest you.
FREDER:	You've already said that.
MARIE:	I hate you.
FREDER:	Good.
MARIE:	Leave the room for God's sake.
FREDER:	That suits you. You're flushed with desire.
MARIE:	I'll leave if you don't go.
FREDER:	Try it.
MARIE:	Do you want to drive me out of my mind?
FREDER:	Yes.
MARIE:	*(To the door.)* I can't stand it.
FREDER:	It's dark in there.
MARIE:	I'll call Mrs Schimmelbrot.
FREDER:	She'll be grateful.
MARIE:	*(Exploding)* I can't bear you any longer.
FREDER:	Caught.
MARIE:	Be quiet or I'll strangle you.
FREDER:	I'm as quiet as a mouse.
MARIE:	If I beg you to?
FREDER:	On your knees.

MARIE: Would you leave me alone?

FREDER: On your knees.

MARIE: *(Kneels)* Leave me alone I implore you.

FREDER: Say the Lord's prayer.

MARIE: God in heaven, I'm going mad.

FREDER: Our father which art in heaven –

MARIE: I can't stand it.

FREDER: Give us this day our daily bread –

MARIE: *(Falls on Freder.)* Out.

FREDER: *(Holds her.)* And forgive us our trespasses –

MARIE: Out.

FREDER: As we forgive them – *(Kisses her.)* You've never looked so lovely.

MARIE: *(Struggles)* I'll strangle you.

FREDER: Rage is catching.

MARIE: Let go.

FREDER: *(Kisses her.)* Say the Lord's prayer and you can die.

MARIE: I'll scream. *(They fall on the bed. She frees herself and flies to Desiree's room.)*

FREDER: *(After her.)* That won't save you. *(Screams. Marie enters and falls onto a stool. Freder appears at the door.)*

MARIE: *(Quiet)* Is it too late?

FREDER: Too late.

MARIE: What should we do with her?

FREDER: Nothing.

MARIE: We should call Alt.

FREDER: Too late.

MARIE: I was with her a minute ago. She made a fool of me.

FREDER: That's the fate of those left behind.

MARIE: She must have taken the veronal before she came to me. How quickly it works!

FREDER: Depends on the quantity.

MARIE: *(Pause)* We should still call a doctor.

FREDER: I made sure.

MARIE: You never know.

FREDER: What for?

MARIE: What for?

FREDER: She'd do it again.

MARIE: What for?

FREDER: Was she cheerful?

MARIE: She was very tired.

FREDER: Was she happy?

MARIE: *(Pause)* I tried to get in, the door was locked. I made a lot of noise before she heard me.

FREDER: She was already half gone.

MARIE: How quick it was.

FREDER: Depends on the amount.

MARIE: Where did she get that much?

FREDER: *(Simply)* I got it for her.

MARIE: *(Quietly)* I'm afraid of you.

FREDER: Shall I leave the room?

MARIE: *(Quickly)* No.

FREDER: You wanted to be left alone.

MARIE: *(Softly)* Murderer.

FREDER: *(Silent)*

MARIE: Why did you get it for her?

FREDER: She would have jumped in the river, otherwise.

MARIE: She might have had time to come to her senses.

FREDER: Because the water's cold?

MARIE:	Because a second later you're sorry.
FREDER:	She was with you after she took it, and wasn't sorry.
MARIE:	*(Pause)* What should we do?
FREDER:	She pleaded with me.
MARIE:	Murderer.
	(Silence)
FREDER:	You have a peculiar fetish for that word.
MARIE:	Little bird. My little sister.
FREDER:	I'll leave you alone.
MARIE:	You'll stay here.
FREDER:	I don't like funeral sermons.
MARIE:	We'll say nothing.
FREDER:	*(Drinks)*
MARIE:	*(Softly)* Me too. *(Pause)* You've brought me to this.
FREDER:	Brought you to what?
MARIE:	Stop pretending.
FREDER:	You're imagining things.
MARIE:	Drink – *(Points at Desiree's door.)* Is the door well locked?
FREDER:	Are you embarrassed?
MARIE:	Drink.
FREDER:	She couldn't hear us anyway.
MARIE:	*(Goes to the door.)* It's locked.
FREDER:	Do you want to sleep with me now?
MARIE:	You know very well.
FREDER:	I don't know.
MARIE:	I'll whisper it in your ear.
FREDER:	*(Avoids her.)* Nobody can hear us.
MARIE:	Don't run away.
FREDER:	Say it.
MARIE:	*(Follows him.)* Are you afraid of me?

FREDER:	I don't understand you.
MARIE:	I won't bite your ear off.
FREDER:	*(Catches her.)* You're not in your right senses.
MARIE:	Maybe.
FREDER:	I'd better go. We should fetch a doctor.
MARIE:	On your knees.
FREDER:	Goodnight.
MARIE:	On your knees.
FREDER:	Marie.
MARIE:	It won't be just the Lord's prayer.
FREDER:	What do you want?
MARIE:	Beg. Doggy wants some sugar? Beg.
FREDER:	You're weird.
MARIE:	I'm wonderful.
FREDER:	Quiet.
MARIE:	I haven't forgotten.
FREDER:	There's a corpse.
MARIE:	Fetishism – Drink. *(Drinks)*
FREDER:	This is madness.
MARIE:	Makes me more enticing. Do you want me?
FREDER:	Stop playing.
MARIE:	Thalatta! Thalatta!
FREDER:	I'm losing my mind.
MARIE:	Thalatta! Thalatta!
FREDER:	*(Wild)* Stop playing. *(After her.)*
MARIE:	*(Laughs)* Catch me. *(Chase)* Catch me. I hate you. You disgust me.
FREDER:	*(Catches)* Not another word.
MARIE:	*(Laughter increases.)* Drink up.
FREDER:	I'm warning you.

MARIE: You're not drunk yet.

FREDER: *(At the door.)* Before I go out of my mind –

MARIE: It's dark in the front room –

FREDER: I'll find my way.

MARIE: You'll knock over a stool.

FREDER: Doesn't matter.

MARIE: Mrs Schimmelbrot will thank you.

FREDER: Something terrible is going to happen.

MARIE: Fetishism.

FREDER: I can't stand you any longer.

MARIE: Caught. *(Tears off her blouse.)* I'm going to bed.

FREDER: Marie.

MARIE: *(Laughing)* I hate you. I despise you. Do you give up?

FREDER: I warn you, it won't be my fault.

MARIE: Our father, which art –

FREDER: *(Wild)* Shut your mouth.

MARIE: Forgive us our trespasses –

FREDER: *(Jumps on her.)*

MARIE: *(Laughing)* Is that all? That's for little boy. *(Escapes)*
            As we forgive those –

FREDER: *(Chases her.)* I'll get you.

MARIE: Come and get me.

FREDER: God forgive us. *(Catches her.)*

MARIE: Who is God? *(Escapes)* You've torn my nice pyjamas.
            Come little boy, come.

FREDER: *(Outraged)* I'm not your little boy. I've lost a shoe.

MARIE: Run, little boy, run.

FREDER: We're not running any more.

MARIE: Little boy can kiss too. Much sweeter. *(Escapes)* You're
            hurting me. He can bite as well – In the neck, little boy.

FREDER: I'm not your little boy.

MARIE:	You'll knock over the table.
FREDER:	*(Throws her onto the bed.)*
MARIE:	Drink first. You haven't drunk enough.
FREDER:	I'm not drinking.
MARIE:	Put the light out. *(Tries to escape.)*
FREDER:	*(Out of his mind.)* Stay put.
MARIE:	I like you. You're strong. Put the light out. *(Runs away.)*
FREDER:	What the hell. Stay right where you are.
MARIE:	*(Puts out the light.)* Here, here, here.
FREDER:	Just try that again.
MARIE:	Never, never. You're strong.
FREDER:	Marie.
MARIE:	*(In agony.)* Murder me. Murder me.

THE END

VARIATION

After the première, Bruckner changed the final scene. The variation begins on page 92 from the fifth line after 'Freder drinks'.

MARIE:	My little sister.
FREDER:	You're right, we should call a doctor.
MARIE:	*(Quickly)* Don't leave me.
FREDER:	As you're afraid of me –
MARIE:	I'm more afraid of being alone.
FREDER:	More than of me – is that possible?
MARIE:	Drink.

FREDER:	*(At the table, drinks.)*
MARIE:	Me too.
FREDER:	*(Pours her a drink.)*
MARIE:	*(Empty)* What will become of me?
FREDER:	If you can ask yourself that you know the answer.
MARIE:	*(Looks at him.)*
FREDER:	The answer is: here's to life, one way or the other.
MARIE:	To life –
FREDER:	Become established at exactly the right moment.
MARIE:	If I think of the corpse.
FREDER:	You were born to become bourgeois. You can't commit suicide. You haven't got it in you.
MARIE:	I just haven't got it in me.
FREDER:	To the general astonishment of all, it appears that even the most gorgeous specimens of the human race have their limitations. On the one hand I need to be taken care of. I don't like work. You, on the other hand like nothing better than working. Indeed, we'll make the perfect pair.
MARIE:	*(Looks at him in despair.)*
FREDER:	It's inevitable. *(At the table, eats.)*
MARIE:	*(Softly)* Help me.
FREDER:	*(With his mouth full.)* You all come to me, one way or the other. Didn't I tell you? But there are some things you have to say more than once before they happen. You couldn't live without me. Without someone to take a hold on things, you all go to pieces.
MARIE:	Help me.
FREDER:	Eat up. Life is to be lived.
MARIE:	*(Begins to cry.)*
FREDER:	I said eat.
MARIE:	*(Crying, starts to eat.)*

THE END